StickMan

The Story of Emmett Chapman and the Instrument He Created

By Jim Reilly

StickMan

First Printing, 2015.
ISBN 978-0-9918729-1-6

Two Handed Press, Calgary, Alberta, Canada.
twohandedpress@gmail.com

The following are Federally registered trademarks of Stick Enterprises, Inc.: Stick, The Stick, Chapman Stick, Grand Stick, Stick Bass, Grid, The Block, and Touchboard.

These and other trademarks belonging to Stick Enterprises Inc. are used throughout this book with permission.

Cover Design and Photography by Dan Chapman
© Chapman Design.

All photos, unless otherwise noted, courtesy of Emmett Chapman and Stick Enterprises.

This book is dedicated to the creative spirit and those with the courage to follow wherever it leads.

(On the right, one of the first hundred Sticks circa 1975. On the left, my graphite 10-string Stick circa 2004.)

Table of Contents

TM

"Music so wishes to be heard that it sometimes calls on unlikely characters to give it voice."

-**Guitar Craft Aphorism***

(*Used with permission, courtesy Robert Fripp/Discipline Global Mobile)

A Message From Tony Levin

Emmett's accomplishments are extraordinary. As an inventor, a manufacturer and a musician, he has re-set boundaries, wowed audiences, and inspired musicians with his abilities. And his engagement in those fields is dynamic – he continues to come up with innovations, to improve the instrument, and to grow as a player.

To those who, like me, are engaged enough with just trying to make music, he stands as an inspiration. And the instrument he gave birth to has given us a new voice, new techniques to explore, and continues to challenge us in the best of ways.

- Tony Levin, March 11, 2015

(Tony Levin in the early '80s leading a Stick workshop in Japan.)

A Note From the Author
(On a plane on my way down to Stick Enterprises)

The first time I travelled down to Stick Enterprises you didn't even really need a passport. If memory serves, I only showed the customs officials my Canadian driver's license and I was on my way.

Today, I'm sitting in a plane making what will most likely be the final trip down before this book is published. This time, I not only had to show my passport, stand in horrendously long lines and take my shoes off as I went through airport screening but I also needed to *officially* list the address I would be staying at while I was in the States. This was a first. Of course I didn't know the *exact* addresses of where I'd be staying, which apparently called national security into question. A few phone calls later, (thankfully the friends and family whose couches I'd be getting to know intimately were all within cell phone range) with addresses clarified and registered with the appropriate people, I was on my way.

What struck me most on my initial voyage, as the plane banked and began its decent into LAX, was the way the San Gabriel Mountains rose up out of the desert and cradled the outstretched metropolis nestled against the Pacific. This time I've made a note to notice that again, and it's a bright, sunny day so that shouldn't be a problem.

On that first trip, I was all nerves. I was going to meet Emmett Chapman (add whatever emphasis you like to impart a naïve sense of reverence). I had started working on this project a few months earlier, but had only talked with Emmett and his wife Yuta on the phone, never face to face. The plane landed, my first time to LAX. I found the car rental place and drove to the hotel. It was really, really hot. My hotel was in Calabasas, about 15 minutes west of Woodland Hills where Emmett lives and works. I called the Chapmans and told them I was on my way. A few minutes later I pulled up to the curb in front of Stick Enterprises.

From the street, Stick Enterprises looks like any other southern California suburban home. Built on the side of a dry, grassy hill, two stories with a narrow deck out front, garage on one side, pool on the other, and an array of indigenous flora and fauna, there's nothing from the outside that would indicate anything other than middle class, West Coast suburbia. I climbed the stairs to the front door and rang the bell. Almost immediately the door opened and I was met by a smiling face and soft German accent, "You must be Jim," said Yuta as she opened the door. "Emmett is on his way down."

There I stood, moments away from meeting one of my heroes, the subject of what would turn into this mountain of work. Questions fought with anticipation for space as my mind raced. Suddenly, there he was – the man who invented The Chapman Stick, the mystery, the riddle I was hoping to solve. He bounded down the stairs to the front foyer, not with a Stick, but with a tennis racquet in hand. "Let's go play," he said.

So, my first face-to-face meeting with Emmett wasn't about music, or the instrument he created, not even stories of his life's journey – we played tennis.

It has been over 10 years since that first meeting and I'm on a plane again. This time I'm travelling from a different Canadian city and with those far stricter travel regulations already mentioned. I'm going down to pick up the last few pieces of the story. What has emerged

8

after all this time? So many questions still. Hopefully by the time I'm done I'll have the answers, but I'm only very cautiously optimistic.

What have I learned so far about Emmett, his work and his music? First, and most importantly, those three things are symbiotically intertwined. One can't be removed from the other two. Emmett's creation and legacy, The Chapman Stick, grew out of a need he had to realize the sounds in his head but it quickly grew into much more than that, not only for Emmett, but also for thousands of musicians around the world.

I asked Nick Beggs (founding member of eighties pop group Kajagoogoo and more recently, Stick player with Led Zeppelin's John Paul Jones and Porcupine Tree's Steven Wilson) what The Stick brought into his life. Firstly, he said, it made him part of a very exclusive club. This is true. It's done that for me too. There aren't a lot of Stick players out there. I've heard New York jazz Stickist Steve Adelson say that playing Stick is almost a spiritual thing. He wouldn't go into more detail, but it is and he's right too. For me, it's simpler though: playing Stick simply feels *right*. There's a naturalness to the way the instrument feels in front of your body and the way both hands engage with each other to make music.

I bought my first Stick directly from Stick Enterprises and when the deal was done Yuta asked me why I had decided to buy one. Even though I had only tentatively tapped a Stick a few rudimentary times when I had very occasionally stumbled across one in a random music store, I knew that The Stick would be the only way to get to the music that I heard in my head. I told her this and she said it made sense.

As I reflect, and I've reflected a lot, what I keep coming back to is that The Stick and being a Stick player has made me special, given me an edge. I was performing a few years ago on a CBC Radio

(Canadian Broadcasting Corporation) show and the host asked me if I was the only Stick player in Kamloops (British Columbia, Canada – the town I was living in at the time). "I prefer to say that I'm the *best* Stick player in Kamloops," I replied. Both were true, she got the joke, but it's more than that. There were thousands of guitar players in Kamloops but no one else played Stick.

Early on I realized that there was no history with this instrument. There were no cool Stick licks to learn like there were when I was first learning guitar. It was all up to me. Every time I picked up my Stick I had the possibility of playing something, of making music that nobody else on the planet had ever made before. I guess that holds true for any instrument but with the millions (billions?) of guitar and bass players out there I find it much more unlikely that you're going to be compared to anyone else when you're playing Stick. With The Stick, it's a new adventure every time.

So what did I uncover through all the research, phone calls, archives, recordings and interviews it took to put together this portrait of the man who started it all? Most importantly, Emmett is first and foremost a musician. Everything he did, everything he created was only to serve the music that he works so passionately and tirelessly to realize. Most surprisingly however, it's not the instrument that makes this story special. Although The Stick is the first thing you see, the first thing you notice, it's the technique Emmett discovered, the way he plays stringed and fretted musical instruments that allowed for all this wonderful music to enter the world. And it all started with a simple tap...

(The author and Emmett, June 2010.)

Chapter 1 – Evolution

The room is silent. The audience has remembered that dimmed house lights signal the beginning of a performance. Quickly, burbling conversations dry up. Attention focuses. In the instant between the end of old banter and the potential to begin anew, a rich baritone voice fills the auditorium from unseen loudspeakers:

"Would You Welcome Please…" (The voice rises ever so slightly. Perhaps this is a question)

"Would you welcome please, Emmett Chapman." The name comes on an exhale, a downbeat. The name is a release. Shoulders drop.

The curtain slowly rises. Red. Applause. The stage, bare and dark, save for a lone figure standing center stage. Four multi-coloured lights create a box, enclosing him. A spotlight illuminates the center of the box and the figure within. He wears a white (at least it appears white from a distance and under the harsh lights) one-piece jumpsuit. It looks like the kind the astronauts wore while training for the Apollo missions.

As the curtain slowly, steadily rises revealing the man's feet, torso, head, a sound washes over the crowd. The sound rises slowly, unhurried, bright, and full like a small river that was once a brook, the brook a few weeks past the heaviest of the spring runoff. The excitement of the coming torrent of water past, this little river, this music, flows strongly, able to handle the steady current now, its banks no longer stretching, but comfortable with the volume.

Sounds flow.

All the while, the man standing center stage seems an enigma. Thinning hair, neat beard, wire rimmed John Lennon glasses speak of maturity, wisdom. A trim, agile body and graceful movements speak of youth and innocence. He has the build of an athlete, maybe a dancer and the hands of a carpenter: thick, strong, confident. Eyes are drawn to his hands. He uses both hands to create the sounds now fully adrift over the crowd. Each hand, each finger determines pitch, volume, expression, tone. One hand chases the other, one steers, the other follows. Both drive confidently ahead together.

He appears at once young and old. His music sounds of confidence and searching but has yet to settle into a specific key; no patterns, no repetitions have emerged.

The man moves. His movement becomes his music. Fluid, strong, now he is a dancer. His head moves, drifts, looks almost like it's floating from side to side. (Does he know it's moving?) The music now has a shape and it looks as it sounds: effortless.

It speeds up.

Is that a theme? Maybe, but now he's off to something else. A pattern? No, it's off somewhere else again.

The music seems to search for itself – unfolding. Will a pattern emerge?

Another exhale. There's the pattern, the key. There's the structure.

All too soon, the sound fades and the music drifts off into the ether.

So went the first minute and a half of Emmett Chapman's performance at *The Soundboard Guitar Concert*, captured on video in the mid-eighties. The back cover of the video case offers a brief description: "*Emmett improvises and plays his originals and standards on the ten strings of the instrument he created, The Stick®. Tapping and holding the strings against an expanded fretboard with the fingers of both hands, he plays orchestrally complete live music - bass, melody, chords and percussion.*"

Some consider The Chapman Stick to be the evolution of the guitar. Others consider it the next step in the history of stringed instruments. That history, though still being defined, reaches back to antiquity.

(Emmett in concert during the '80s.)

If the first human musical instrument was the voice and the second was two relatively solid objects struck together, the third must have been some sort of stretched string fixed to two solid points and strummed, plucked or hit. Paintings on ancient Egyptian tombs date the earliest versions of the harp to around 3000 BC. Versions of

14

primitive harps have been found in Europe, Asia and Africa. The first stringed instrument to be bowed rather than plucked like a harp is believed to be the rebec, also known as the ribible. Mention of this instrument can be found in "The Miller's Tale" from Chaucer's *Canterbury Tales* dating back to the end of the 14th century. The most obviously guitar-like instruments first appeared in earnest in 16th century Spain[1], and quickly became popular among the middle and lower classes – an instrument for the people. Portable and relatively easy to play, or at least to make sound reasonably good, the guitar quickly spread across Europe. By the middle of the 18th century it had morphed into the acoustic guitar we recognize today: six strings, a curved body shape and internal bracing. Guitars in all sonic ranges from treble to contrabass appeared before the end of the 19th century.

The 20th century added electricity to the equation. Originally, in a battle merely to be heard above drums, saxophones and trumpets, instrument builders, players and electronic tinkerers simply modified hollow body acoustic guitars. All sorts of strategies were tried to amplify the sound. In 1931, the Electro String Instrument Corporation, more specifically Adolph Rickenbacker and George Beauchamp, manufactured guitars with tungsten pickups. These pickups could transfer the acoustic vibration of the strummed or plucked guitar strings into an electric signal, which could then be amplified enough in volume to compete with other instruments in the popular bands of the day. Guitarists could now be heard and they quickly took center stage.

The first recording of an amplified guitar solo is believed to be Eddie Durham's solo on "Hittin' the Bottle" with The Jimmy

---

[1] Although images on Hittite sculptures found in North Syria depict very guitar-like stringed and fretted musical instruments dating around 1500 BC. The early Spanish guitars are widely cited as the precursor to today's guitar.

Lunceford Big Band. On the recording, Lunceford grabbed the microphone and stuck it in front of Durham's guitar, making it stand out above the rest of the band. On stage, Durham used a guitar with a pickup built in to achieve the same effect. Two years later, Charlie Christian would become the world's first electric guitar superstar, stealing the spotlight from the other soloists night after night with the Benny Goodman orchestra. In the December 1939 issue of *Downbeat* magazine, Christian is quoted as saying, "Amplifying my instrument has made it possible for me to get a wonderful break. A few weeks ago, I was working for beans down in Oklahoma, having a plenty tough time of getting along and playing the way I wanted to play. So take heart, all you starving guitarists—I know that you play damned fine music, but now you've got a chance to bring the fact to the attention of not only short-sighted band leaders, but to the attention of the world."

While these early, amplified hollow body guitars were good, they weren't great. Guitars were temperamental and would feedback at loud volumes. Les Paul took major strides towards solving this problem in 1941 when he created the first widely known solid body electric guitar. He dubbed it 'The Log.' Without the resonating top found on hollow, fully acoustic instruments, a solid body guitar could be played at much louder volumes and take on the characteristics of the amplifier as well as the guitar and strings. As an added bonus, the electric guitar pickup could be much more powerful in a solid body guitar, which translated into a lighter, faster, easier playing instrument.

Leo Fender, previously an amplifier maker, completed the evolution to the electric guitar in 1950 with the release of the Fender Broadcaster. The Broadcaster and its companion, the Fender Esquire, were affordable, mass-produced electric guitars that immediately grabbed the attention of the masses. The Broadcaster was renamed the Telecaster in 1951, due to a trademark dispute with the Gretsch drum company. In 1952, realizing Fender's success, Gibson released its own solid body electric guitar designed by Ted McCarty and named after Les Paul. The Telecaster and Les Paul, along with Fender's Stratocaster, set the standard and created the blueprint for today's electric guitars. Not only did they define the instrument, but they also led and continue to lead musicians to uncover new music. Without the Les Paul, the Strat, or even the Gibson SG, Jimmy Page, Jimi Hendrix, Angus Young and millions of other guitarists would all be very different musicians.

Shortly after the Broadcaster, Fender brought the world of solid bodies and electric pickups to the bass guitar. Much like the acoustic guitar, acoustic bass guitars had been crudely amplified for years when Fender introduced the solid body Precision Bass in 1951. Lloyd Loar is credited with, in 1926, building the first amplified upright bass and Rickenbacker made a streamlined version of an electric upright in 1936. But it wasn't until the Fender Precision that the full potential, versatility, volume and playability of the bass guitar matched that of the electric guitar. And as had been the case with the guitar, the electric bass paved the way for the birth of the superstar bass guitarist.

By contrast, the modern piano has a comparatively shorter history than that of the guitar. It too evolved from earlier instruments. Around 250 BC, a Greek engineer named Ctesibius of Alexandria created an instrument with keys and levers that opened and closed valves controlling the flow of air across a series of pipes much like today's church organs. Organs developed through the ages. Their biggest advantage over stringed instruments was the wide range of pitches available, from very low to very high on one instrument. The biggest disadvantage was their size. Low notes meant big pipes. You had to go to the instrument, the instrument couldn't come to you. Sitting around the campfire with a church organ was out of the question.

The piano grew out of the harp and through the harpsichord. The harpsichord merged a set of keys that operated a series of levers that in turn plucked individual strings. You could pluck short, thin, high-pitched strings and long, fat, low-pitched strings. You could also play with both hands. Music became more and more complex and self-sufficient. A single musician could now play chords, scales, melodies and accompaniment at the same time on a single instrument that could fit in a modestly sized room. The only thing missing from the harpsichord was dynamics. The strings were all plucked with the same velocity; hence all sounded at the same volume regardless of how hard one struck the keys.

Enter Bartolomeo Cristofori's 'loud-soft' machine, the pianoforte, which was later shortened in name to the piano. Cristofori's piano replaced the pluck of the harpsichord with hammers that struck each string. Between the key and the hammered string, the series of levers and mechanics was much more complicated than the harpsichord's, but those mechanics enabled dynamics. The result was an instrument that covered almost the entire useable range of pitches and that could be played loudly, quietly or any step in-between. The pianist could evoke all sorts of emotion with the tap of a finger and the press of a key.

New musical instruments are rare. New musical innovations that catch the attention of creative musicians and lead to dynamic, new, engaging music are rarer still. The five choices in Howard Goodall's book *Big Bangs: The Story of Five Discoveries That Changed Musical History,* are prefaced with the following stipulation: "changes to music that happened in one place at one time: one day the invention wasn't there, the next it was." This ruled out symphonic music or instruments like the violin, both of which evolved slowly over centuries.

In 1969, a Los Angeles musician experienced a history-making musical moment. One instant the discovery wasn't there. The next, the potential for not only music but also for an entirely new instrument capable of realizing that music, lay before him. In an instant, and with no real forethought, Emmett Chapman played his guitar like he had never played it before. Others had come close to doing what he did, but in that split second, Emmett went further than anyone else and leapt into uncharted waters. Immediately, he knew he was on to something good.

From that moment of inspired discovery in 1969, a new musical instrument was born. Following Goodall's edict above, we have to go back to Adolph Sax in the late nineteenth century to find the previous inventor who successfully created a new musical instrument with a lasting social impact. Beyond that we need to go back, with smaller stops along the way, to Bartolomeo Cristofori's pianoforte. Sax's saxophone, the piano and now Emmett's instrument, The Chapman Stick all involved a shift. That shift may have seemed radical at the time, but in hindsight, can be seen as an inevitable reflection and evolution directly resulting from those specific musical times. These shifts altered people's perceptions of how sound can be created, manipulated and maintained. Rather than merely offering a new tonal palette for the musician to explore, as with the modern day sound synthesizers, Emmett's realization in 1969 brought forth a new way for the musician to interact with, to control, to converse with his instrument.

In its simplest terms, Emmett discovered that rather than strumming or plucking the strings of his guitar, he could tap the strings against the frets with both hands. The way he tapped and what he did after that though, was anything but simple. Following the discovery of his unique two-handed tapping technique, Emmett continued to modify his electric guitar to fully capitalize on the potential of both hands tapping. No longer did the guitarist have to pluck or strum the string with one hand and determine the pitch of the string with the other. Each finger, each tap on the string created pitch, dynamics, rhythm, tone and expression. What evolved was a marriage of the guitar, bass guitar, piano and even percussion, but the whole was greater than the sum of its parts. As Emmett's instrument evolved into the ultimate tool to express his music, so too did Emmett. Within five years, the modified guitar became an entirely new instrument: first named The Electric Stick, then The Chapman Stick. Emmett became a fulltime musician. Others quickly became fascinated with the music, the man making this new music and the instrument itself. In response to others' requests, he started making instruments for other players and by 1974, he started his own company, Stick Enterprises Inc., to manufacture, distribute and promote The Stick.

At the heart of Emmett's story and at the heart of The Stick's story is music. Music has always been Emmett's driving force and reason for creating, evolving, refining and playing The Stick. This is the story of a man who followed a passion, faced unbelievable odds, stuck to his beliefs and convictions, and found his place in the world. Along the way, Emmett continued to realize his musical vision, inspire musicians of all ranks and even fight off attacks to his

20

credibility, business and his very claim to the technique he created and developed. While the story of the music is still playing itself out from world-renowned concert stages to small basement bedrooms, Emmett's story, and therefore by default, the story of The Stick, started back in Italy, many, many years ago.

Chapter 2 – From Pardee to Chapman

"There's a story that goes with this photo. It's my Italian grandfather's mother, from Bari, in Southern Italy."

Photos are spread out over what used to be the kitchen table. The kitchen table which doubles (triples) as a workbench, study, even a place to eat meals, now serves as the plinth, framing countless photographs, countless memories. We are pouring over these photos, diving off each one into another memory, another tale.

Emmett continues, "So the story is this: Her name is Grazia Lorette. My mother always described her as 'The Terror of the Village.' She would grab my grandfather by his ear and drag him back home. She was a very tough, rugged woman."

The photograph before us confirms the description.

"So when our daughter Grace was born in Germany, we picked a classic name 'Grace' but couldn't come up with a second name. I think I told you this on the phone?" Emmett directs the question towards me. But I don't remember him telling me the story before.

"So I thought of Grace Loraine as a nice rhythm, but Loraine wasn't in the name book, the German/English name book in the German hospital. So I picked the one next to it: 'Loretta.'

"And you didn't even know about Grazia Lorette?" Emmett's brother Dan asks incredulously. (I love the interplay between the brothers.)

"I didn't think of even Grace linking with Grazia Lorette. Both names, by coincidence, turned out to be the names of her Great Grandmother. No, her Great-Great-Grandmother.

So these are shots…"

Dan's not ready to move on. "That's amazing that you didn't make the connection, that you weren't aware of it."

"Let's see, yeah, the way it happened kind of illustrates that we weren't aware of it." Despite Dan's best efforts Emmett has moved on. "This one is me, I was raised in Florida. And that's my mom, I was four..."

Much of Grazia Lorette's toughness and ruggedness lives on in Emmett's daughter, Grace. Grace has her father's hands. She too is a musician and now works beside Emmett making Chapman Sticks. There is a long line of strong, rugged, independent women in Emmett's life. I doubt Grazia was the first. The line continues down through Emmett's mother, wife and daughters. This fiery Italian blood comes through Emmett too, although it runs a little further below the surface.

On the map, Bari sits just where the heel of Italy's famous boot starts. It's a port city, facing the Adriatic, on the edge of the Terra di Bari plateau. Modern day Bari is divided into two parts: the old city with its medieval streets, monuments and churches and the more modern section, developed after 1820. The Corso Vittorio Emanuele marks the dividing line between the old and the new. Bari has a long and rich history. Historians date the city's founding to somewhere around 150 BC. However, an ancient population called the Japigi has left records of its existence around Bari, which date back to the 1st Millennium BC. Countless wars have been waged for control of the rich, beautiful, economically beneficially situated port town. The Byzantines, the Normans, the house of Svevi, the Angioini, the Spanish, Austrians and the Bourbons all laid claim to the town. Finally, in 1860, Bari was unified with the rest of the kingdom of

Italy. Throughout this time, Bari was coveted for its ports, its easy access to the rest of the Mediterranean and its fiery population. These days, some Italians call Bari "The California of the South." They say it's far more progressive, more active and much more commercially competitive than other southern cities.

In the late 1800's Grazia Lorette's son, Giuseppe DiCosola left Bari and headed for the United States. He ended up in Chicago, Illinois, turned Giuseppe into Joe and set out to make a future for himself. Joe DiCosola could run and sing. They called him Joe the Wind and Joe the Singer. Within his community he was both respected and feared. He worked on the railroad and was recognized as being hardworking and trustworthy. Other Italian immigrants would come to him with their money, so he created a bank to manage it. A natural entrepreneur, in addition to a bank, he owned a racetrack and cheese factories. Joe eventually became sheriff of the county.

These were the days when the Mafia ran Chicago and there are stories of run-ins with the mob. Joe's daughter Venetia tells of mob extortion or 'black hand' letters threatening her father and the family. Once, someone tried to break into the DiCosola house by cutting through a window with a diamond cutter. Joe stood his ground and the intruder disappeared into the night. He hid Mafia informants in the house. One day, a 'black hand' letter arrived at the house with a skull and crossbones on it. The threat was clear. Joe was supposed to show up on a specified street corner that evening. Heroically and defiantly, he showed up at the intersection and sat on a trashcan with two six shooters across his chest. The mob car pulled up, saw Joe and drove off in the opposite direction.

While working for the railroad, Joe married Jessie Reibel. She was the daughter of a Swiss immigrant of German and French ancestry and played a Hohner harmonica. They ended up in South Dakota. On April 24, 1912 in Aberdeen, South Dakota, their daughter Venetia, Emmett's mother, was born. The family soon moved back to Chicago and put down roots.

There was no shortage of music in the DiCosola house. Venetia and her brother, also named Joe, played guitars and sang along with Joe Sr. Joe Sr. loved opera and young Venetia would perform the classics for her father. Her voice better suited folk music and jazzier tunes however, and she gravitated towards those genres with the passion of a true performer. Although Venetia attended both the Art Institute of Chicago and a school for beauticians, music and performing were her passions. While still a teenager, she would take her guitar and walk into clubs on Chicago's Rush Street and simply start playing. One of two things inevitably happened: she would either leave with her guitar case full of cash from appreciative club patrons, or the club itself would hire her. She crashed every club on Rush Street. She was the real deal. Her act was solid, and when she went into that act, more often than not, people were captivated. She knew songs in Italian, Spanish, Russian, Gypsy and English and would modify her show for just about any audience in the ethnically and culturally diverse Chicago clubs of the day.

Emmett's father, Emmett Pardee Sr. was born in Port Townsend, Washington, on November 9th, 1909, the second son of Medora Small and James Pardee. James Pardee was born in Micanopy, Florida on March 18th, 1877 and died in 1968 in Santa Barbara, California. He was the son of Levi Pardee and Rebecca Croxton. Small and Pardee were married June 30th, 1907 in Everett, Washington. James Pardee worked as a telegraph operator and railroad worker.

The Pardee's was a religious house, and young Emmett Pardee was drawn into the excitement, passion, fervour and showmanship of the revivalist minister. Pardee became a traveling minister himself with the Church of Universal Reconciliation. Universal Reconciliation is a Christian sect, whose doctrine revolves around the belief that anyone, regardless of his or her faith, can receive salvation due to the love and mercy of God. It's a syncretistic belief, a blending of different belief systems into something new. Specific virtues and salvation aren't directly linked to Jesus however. Universal Reconcilists struggle with the belief that only righteous and virtuous Christians will avoid Hell and enter the Kingdom of Heaven. If the mainstream church sees its job as ensuring the salvation of those already included within the church, then Universalists view their role as ministers to reconcile the rest of humanity. Salvation is available to all, and while the process of salvation may differ for everyone, the ultimate result will be the bringing together and deliverance of all humanity. "Once Saved Always Saved" is their slogan, but there is a definite element of predisposition. If God is truly omnipotent then He already knows whether or not one is headed for Heaven or Hell.

Venetia was raised Catholic by her Italian father in an Italian neighbourhood in Chicago. They would watch the Catholic Parade of Saints make its way in full regalia down the city streets. Her patron saint was Saint Teresa of Avila. All this would change when she was in her late teens and heard the Chicago based, Christian fundamentalist *Moody Bible Institute Radio Show*. Listening every week to the show's host James L. Gray led to a complete change of heart. She accepted the fundamentalist Protestant belief that Jesus was her saviour far more fervently than she had while in the Catholic

Church. She was redeemed, her soul was saved through evangelical religion and she needed to go out and save other people's souls.

Around the same time as Venetia was being saved in Chicago, Emmett Pardee loaded up his truck, with signs on the side that read in bold, block letters: *"THERE IS NO DIFFERENCE FOR ALL HAVE SINNED AND COME SHORT OF THE GLORY OF GOD"²* and *"THIS IS A FAITHFUL SAYING, AND WORTHY OF ALL ACCEPTATION, THAT CHRIST JESUS CAME INTO THE WORLD TO SAVE SINNERS."³* He hit the road, taking his message of salvation through God's love and mercy for all across the country. Pardee's travelling ministry rolled into Chicago. Venetia went to his revival tent meeting and fell head over heels in love with the exciting, fiery sermons and the young man delivering them. On July 5th, 1935, Emmett and Venetia married and settled down in Santa Barbara, California.

(Emmett Pardee and his travelling ministry.)

---

² Romans 2:32
³ 1 Timothy 1:15

For Venetia, Santa Barbara felt like heaven. In her diary she wrote that life was totally harmonious. She was happy with her religion and with her husband's role as minister. She wanted the good things to keep coming and never change. Soon Emmett Sr. gave up the travelling ministry and took a job with the phone company, but he was still able to lead his own church. A year after settling down, on September 28th, 1936, their son Emmett Howard Pardee Jr. was born. Later, Venetia would contradict those early feelings of perfection and say that she felt very guilty about Emmett Sr. giving up his travelling ministry and settling down to raise a family; however at the time everything seemed perfect.

The 1930s were difficult times in the United States and around the world. The Great Depression and its aftermath threw many into poverty and caused tremendous struggles for individuals and families alike. These struggles didn't escape the young Pardee family. Shortly after Emmett Jr.'s birth, the Pardees started receiving alarming letters from Venetia's mother, who had relocated to Florida. The letters spoke of great hardships and conveyed a sense of emergency. Her mother was in trouble and she asked Venetia to go to Florida and help.

From the outset, Emmett Sr. didn't want Venetia to go and told her to choose between her mother and him. Venetia went to Florida, not believing Emmett Sr.'s ultimatum. But true to his threat, when things had settled down enough to allow her to return, Emmett refused to accept her back. In 1937, a year after Emmett Jr.'s birth, the Pardees separated permanently and would later divorce.

For the next three years Emmett Jr. and his mother lived in a run down, one room shack they shared with their mother/grandmother

Jesse Reibel in Largo, Florida. Today, Largo is a vibrant city of over 77,000, but when young Emmett lived there it was a seriously economically depressed town of only 1,500.

(A young Emmett in Florida.)

Their shack was incredibly small and sat in the middle of swampy, rural Florida lowland. "It was hardly bigger than a chicken shack," says Emmett. The inside walls were just the wooden framing, chicken wire and tarpaper. They had no running water. The walls were all black with only two small windows, one cut just above a kitchen sink. There were scorpions in the house and rattle snakes in the yard. Not surprisingly, Grandma was always harping on young Emmett about the dangers of snakes, fires and other hazards. Sepia toned photographs show a young, forlorn Emmett sitting outside at a water pump. There's little water anywhere though. The ground is parched and dusty with only tufts of grass and low lying bushes dotting the desolate landscape. Another photo shows a much happier

Emmett, still with the same bleak background, scorched earth and spotty greenery. This time he's standing up, holding onto his mother's guitar. The guitar is taller than the straw-hatted child, but the look of joy on his face is unmistakable.

(Emmett and his mom's guitar.)

The family was exceedingly poor. Emmett talks of eating only oatmeal for days on end. They had no milk, often no salt and very little else. From time to time his mother would go oyster fishing. The oysters were a rare treat and "extraordinarily delicious," says Emmett.

In Florida, Venetia regularly performed her music at the St. Petersburg Yacht Club and sang for soldiers at a nearby army base. She also sang in Spade Cooley's country and western band. Cooley would become quite successful in the 1950s with his own television variety show. He offered her a permanent spot in his band, but she turned him down because she actually disliked country and western music.

Emmett Sr. completely cut himself off from Emmett Jr. and his ex-wife. Save for letters back and forth regarding child support, the three had no meaningful contact for years. When Emmett was six, he and his mother went to San Francisco where Emmett Sr. was living at the time. He had just returned from active duty in WWII fighting in the South Pacific. Emmett Jr. says, "When I saw him he was in a little apartment and he seemed kind of like a tragic figure in a way, very reticent, almost shy, not communicative. Then when he was driving us back to where we were staying, my mother was crying so loud, he pretty much pushed us out of the car in the middle of traffic, and left us in the middle of the street." Father and son wouldn't meet again until Emmett Jr. was an adult.

Jessie, Venetia and Emmett moved around Florida for a couple of years. Eventually Emmett and his mom went up to Chicago and stayed for a few weeks with colourful Italian father, Joe. The two then continued on to California where Venetia met Ulysses Laverne Chapman.

Ulysses Laverne Chapman was born in the small mid-west town of Moweaqua, Illinois, right outside of Decatur. He came from a big family, ten kids in all, but only one was a full biological brother, the rest were stepsiblings. Venetia met Laverne while he was standing in front of a downtown Los Angeles movie theatre. She was handing out gospel tracts for an LA Mission that was associated with Aimee Semple McPherson and her Foursquare Pentecostal Church[4]. Chapman was in front of the theatre tearing up his movie tickets. Venetia went up to him and asked him what was wrong. Chapman

---

[4] McPherson started the Foursquare Pentecostal Church in Los Angeles in 1927, building the Church's largest temple, the Angelus Temple, there.

told her that he was waiting for a date, but that she had stood him up. The two made small talk, he took one of her tracts and left. A short while later, Venetia was heading home, when a man suddenly pulled up beside her in a car and started harassing her. The stranger began to get aggressive and was insistent that she get into his car with him. Meanwhile, Chapman was standing in a nearby doorway, saw what was going on and stepped in to save her.

Venetia and Emmett moved back to California permanently in 1942 to be with Laverne Chapman. In 1943 Laverne and Venetia married. The family settled in Roscoe, now called Sun Valley, in the San Fernando Valley. Laverne officially adopted Emmett and Emmett Howard Pardee Jr. became Emmett Howard Chapman. He was eight.

Chapter 3 – Growing up in Sunny SoCal

Another phone call, more stories. Emmett's told me this one a couple of times now. Each time I can hear a sparkle in his voice. Perhaps this is where it all started...

"I also remember when I was three and a half or four," he says. "I must have been four. I went with my mother to a courtroom, downtown in St. Petersburg, to see a judge. He was looking at her correspondence with my father. It was about final divorce papers, which Emmett Pardee wanted. He wanted to be finished with the whole thing and be divorced. She was crying, and very emotional about it. The judge asked me all kinds of questions and I gave him these long, elaborate answers. He had a strange voice, I remember it sound like he was way off in the distance and it sounded like he was speaking through a radio or had something in his throat. He'd say, "Brilliant child! What a brilliant child!" After everything I'd say, he'd have a response like that, and it affected me. I guess he made me believe it."

Like the family Laverne grew up in, these new Chapmans were a blended family. Laverne had two sons, Jerry and Ronny, from a previous marriage. Ronny was three years younger than Jerry and Jerry was two years younger than Emmett. Five years separated the three boys. Their first house was on Satsuma Street, in Roscoe. The chain link fence in the backyard separated the Chapman property from the Lockheed Aircraft Company. The boys would watch the planes and the first fighter jets come in and take off. Fighter planes and bombers were regular highlights. The kids had the run of the land.

They were left to their own devices to roam with other neighbourhood children and explore the trees, streams, hills and valleys of the new community. On July 11, 1951, Venetia gave birth to a son they named Daniel. Dan was 15 years younger than Emmett, and although Emmett would leave home when Dan was only three, the two would go on to have profound impacts on each other's lives.

(Emmett and brother Dan. Photo courtesy of Dan Chapman)

Both the move back to California and Venetia's marriage to Laverne brought stability into everyone's life. Venetia and Laverne were intent on raising a family, living in a suburban neighbourhood and doing things the middle-class American way. Laverne became *Dad* to Emmett, and set to work becoming the faithful, dependable breadwinner. Venetia was the homemaker and both parents vowed to treat all the boys "fair and square." "We're all a family now," they would say.

(Laverne Chapman.)

Laverne worked hard for his family. He had a work ethic that bordered on the extreme and he often held down multiple jobs. During the Depression he worked in a Civilian Conservation Corps work camp[5]. After the Depression he got a labourer's job with the heavy machine building company Caterpillar and later got jobs with both Bendix Aviation and the U.S. Post Office. He would do his regular job at Bendix, come home, eat and sleep for a few hours, wake up at 3 a.m., go to the post office for the morning shift and then go straight back to his day job at Bendix. He kept up this pace until his youngest son Dan had left the house.

---

[5] Franklin D. Roosevelt formed the Civilian Conservation Corps (CCC) for unemployed young men during the Depression as a means to offer financial aid in return for physical labour on State and Municipal projects. Conditions in the CC weren't easy. The work was hard, the food substandard, workers lived in camps, wore uniforms, and lived with a very military like regime.

Emmett worked hard too, trying to live up to Laverne's standards. Laverne was strict but fair, a hardworking man of few words, who raised four children and in his later years, nursed Venetia through a serious degenerative illness. Whereas Venetia was the outgoing, outspoken entertainer, traits that he greatly admired in his wife, Laverne was non-demonstrative and self-effacing. True to his Midwest, small-town upbringing, Laverne believed in getting by with as few words as possible, never putting oneself out in front, never bragging. He considered bragging to be almost a cardinal sin.

Laverne brought sports, geography, a love of knowledge and a spirit of intuitive play into Emmett's life. "He was like an athlete trying to read an opponent's mind," says Emmett. "He taught me the luxury of 'spin' in life. Spin of the cue ball, spin of the basketball, spin of the Ping-Pong ball, spin of the bowling ball. He did all those things, and I learned how to do them too. There's something deeply symbolic about 'spin,' even on a molecular level. It's something you don't normally consider when you think of travelling from point A to point B. It's not in the manual of how to live one's life but it's what makes things work. It's magic. He taught me that. Some things in life are intuitive, some things are counterintuitive, but make all the difference. My Dad taught me that and it's become second nature."

The two didn't always see eye-to-eye though. "He'd get mad at me because I wouldn't do things the conventional way," says Emmett. "He thought that I couldn't operate my hands properly. I didn't operate with the team. I was not a team player. He didn't like that. But I tried to explain to him that I was exploring, was trying to figure out how to do whatever I was doing the best way possible. Looking back on it, I was searching for a method in everything I did, and wouldn't be satisfied with just doing things the way everyone else did – even as a kid. It was an urge to invent my own world, invent my own culture and invent a way of seeing and responding to everything strictly on my own terms because I felt alienated from any culture." Even as a child and youngster growing up, Emmett created his own sense of purpose and became his own driving force.

(Emmett, Venetia, Jerry and Ronny on Woodlake, November 1946.)

The Chapman's was a religious house, with Sunday and Wednesday night prayer meetings at their Pentecostal Church and Bible study groups on Thursday evenings for the boys. Emmett memorized Bible verses and won prizes. It was a time of soul searching for the growing boy. Often Venetia sought out tiny churches that were just starting out. "Some weren't even competent churches," Emmett says. "She was rebellious, even within her religion." Their Foursquare Pentecostal Church revolved around letting go and giving oneself over to the Holy Spirit. Usually reserved, conservative, white, middle-class adults would be jumping up and down, falling on the floor, speaking in tongues, losing control and letting the Holy Spirit completely take over. Emmett's brother Dan believes that both he and Emmett have hung onto that need to loosen up the analytical, left brain control and engage the creative, intuitive right brain but the desire to lose their self-consciousness and be free came through music and art rather than religion.

Venetia brought her music into the Chapman's house. Her brother Joe would often come over with his guitar, and brother and sister would sing their songs well into the evening. When he was thirteen, Emmett's grandmother gave him an accordion: his first, very own, musical instrument. Although music was just one of many things in young Emmett's life, he threw himself into it with the same enthusiasm and energy that he approached everything else. The only music lessons Emmett ever took were from a woman at his church, Sister Ruth Moodie. She played the piano in church and would sometimes play the organ if the congregation was using a different building and there was an organ there. Emmett says, "She was like an angel, a beautiful lady, dignified and totally quiet. She'd never say anything, never offer opinions. She'd just sit there with a quiet dignity."

Emmett quickly became competent and comfortable enough to play his accordion in public. He was soon performing for his church's congregation and at home for houseguests. From the outset, he was putting his own twist on the music he played by coming up with original arrangements of well-known hymns and standards. From the beginning, Emmett added his personality, his originality to create his own music.

(Emmett on accordion with brothers Ron and Jerry.)

Shortly after his first accordion performances, he began playing what he calls "one-handed piano" in the Chapman's church. Emmett played the piano accordion style, with his right hand playing chords. He soon added one-finger bass lines with his left hand, on the lower notes of the piano. Chords fascinated him. He discovered that chords created harmony. From the chord, the melody and rhythms drew their relevance for the young musician. He discovered that the same note played against different chords had drastically different sounds and musical implications. In Emmett's own words, "chords gave depth and meaning to melody." The chords on the accordion and church piano gave Emmett full control over the depth and meaning of the melody notes.

BACK ROW—T. Powell, V. Lee, Mr. Brown, W. Videtsky, K. Volz, V. Rall, A. Rowley, S. MacPherson, P. McMeen, C. Lowery, G. Linneman, R. Meredith, B. Lunstrum, J. Nickols.
FRONT ROW—W. Dameron, Business Manager, G. Briggs, Co-Editor, P. Martin, Assitant Editor, E. Chapman, Co-Editor, D. Wright, Editor Reseda News, Hunters' Call.

(Editor Emmett at Canoga Park Sr. High.)

In junior and senior high school, Emmett was both academic and athletic. He ran cross-country, wrote and edited both the John Sutter Jr. High paper, *The 49er* and the Canoga Park Sr. High School student newspaper, *The Hunter's Call*. He wrote a column for the high school paper called *Psymple Psychology*. He drew portraits and characters and created posters and other visual arts for the school. Emmett played basketball, tennis, swam, dove and was just as busy outside of school. Emmett and his father built the Chapman's second San Fernando Valley home, in Woodland Hills.[6] He can and did move in almost every direction, all with more or less equal success.

40

"The [San Fernando] Valley was in transition from being rural to being part of a very bustling city," says Bill Ketteman, Emmett's friend since high school. "It was a collection of small towns. Canoga Park and Woodland Hills were the first two separate cities and it was very much rural. Warner Brothers had their big ranch there. We could still safely ride our bicycles on Ventura Boulevard, which ran the length of the valley. We spent a lot of time at the beach and at the half a dozen theatres that were nearby. For 50 cents we could catch artsy foreign films at the Sherman Theatre or get a cheap seat on Wednesdays at the Hollywood Bowl."

Staying busy was Emmett's saving grace. "It took me out of my own psychology – which wasn't working so well," he says. "Mentally, I was good. Physically, I was good – strong at both of those. Philosophically, as a form of mental fitness, I excelled. Emotionally though, anyone could outlast me. I had to get away. That was my makeup."

Much like his biological father, who Venetia used to say couldn't handle the simplest of arguments. "At the first sign of conflict Emmett Sr. would say things like, 'simmer down now,' or he'd just walk away. He would walk away backwards, just back off," she says. Emmett Jr. inherited some of his father's tendencies, but balanced those with his grandfather's ability to remain incredibly concentrated and sustain an argument's intensity for hours. Those contradicting traits were often at odds with each other.

"Emmett would stick with an interest way beyond what, for me, would have been reasonable or expected," says Ketteman, "but he would get somewhere with it. That's what he did with each of his

---

6 The house still stands, only a couple of blocks away from where Emmett lives and works today. The Chapmans had one more Valley home, a few miles away, in Northridge.

interests. He was rather quiet about it, but as he talked about these different topics, it was clear that he was serious about them in positive ways. He wasn't doubtful or negative. None of that. He was optimistic and hopeful. When we talked, what I would say back to him seemed to create more interest in those thoughts and he'd improve on them. We had similar, broad interests. We'd sit together at lunch and chat about the world events, topics big and small. I had a lot of respect for his views. I felt that we were similar in that respect, but he would take it further and surprise me by inevitably making something out of what we were talking about when I thought he wasn't getting anywhere."

The move back to California and Venetia's marriage to Laverne brought stability into Emmett's life, but this stability was built on a foundation of change. Emmett though, would embrace changes, would seek them out. When he talks of his childhood, Emmett mentions that the one constant was the compulsion to change. While change may reflect instability, this does not ring true for Emmett. Nor does the idea that change occurs only for its own sake. Emmett says that, as a child, he saw no difference between sports, music, academics, psychology or any of the other things that occupied his time. They were all challenges, things that had to be done. Emmett calls them all "active and positive" activities, rather than merely distractions to keep busy. No single pursuit was more important than any other. The young Emmett favoured action over talk, choosing to act rather than to contemplate his actions.

Emmett graduated from high school and left the family house when he was 17, with big plans to travel Europe and become a journalist. He liked to write and his philosophical nature allowed him to see the bigger picture. At the time, there were no inclinations to play music professionally. That would have to wait for a few years, when he was a senior at UCLA and needed a way to get out of his graveyard shift operating a drill press at Bendix Aviation.

Chapter 4 – Intrepid Young Traveller to Family Man

"I was just leaving Edinburgh for Glasgow, to take the steamer to Belfast, Ireland when a man with a pipe grabbed me and asked me my name. I told him to beat it, but he kept at me. I began to mildly shoo him off, but it did no good. Then I got mad and was just in the process of measuring the distance from my fist to his jaw when two bobbies approached. I was relieved, but not for long. It turned out that he was a plain-clothes policeman who thought that he had really nabbed me with the goods. But what goods – where – goods?? I was very much confused."

-Letter from Emmett to his Mom and Dad, published in the Canoga Park News, *1955.*

(Our 'Intrepid Young Traveller' was all right. His run-in with the local law enforcement was a case of mistaken identity. A trip back to the hostel and a look at Emmett's passport proved that he wasn't the criminal the bobbies were hunting.)

Emmett's graduation from Canoga Park High School in 1954 was an emotional time for the whole family. Emmett had become a father figure to his younger brother Dan but he had no intentions of sticking around LA. Immediately after graduation he made plans to hitchhike across the U.S. to New York and then travel on to Europe with his high school friend, Chuck Hunt.

"I remember standing in the Lutheran Church parking lot in Woodland Hills and Emmett telling me that he was going to go to Europe," says Bill Ketteman. "I was immediately full of questions and doubts about the whole enterprise. He said that he was going to go down to one of the main routes, Route 66 probably, so that he could hitchhike to New York. Apparently he had a bag and that was just about it. I was doubtful, but he did it!"

"Just before graduation we were standing in a little circle of friends, talking about what we were going to do after we graduated," adds Emmett's traveling companion, Chuck Hunt. "My dad wanted me to go to college and get an engineering degree and I was going in that direction, but then Emmett said that he was going to travel around Europe. After the group broke up I went over to him and said, 'Man, I'd like to do that with you' and that was it – we decided to go together."

Emmett stayed true to his word. He made his way across the States, arrived in New York and immediately started working and saving money. He worked in the mailroom of the American Radiator and Standard Sanitary Corporation at 39 West 39th St. All the while, plans for the trek across the Atlantic took shape.

"We didn't hitchhike together," Chuck continues. "He went to New York City and got that office job. I got a job at a factory in Glendale while he was in New York making his money. I hopped a Greyhound bus to get out there. We were to meet in New York. He gave me an address. I got off the bus in New York City, had never been there before and had no idea where I was or where on earth the address was where I was supposed to meet Emmett. I had no money for a taxi. I started walking in the direction I thought his apartment was in, in this massive complex of people and I bumped into him on the street. He was coming the other way and we walked right into each other. It was amazing. Everything just seemed to fall into place like that."

"He wrote me from New York," says Ketteman, "and said that he had to find work, so he took a crumby job in a mailroom right downtown. It was really noisy and his boss yelled at him because he was too slow and he thought he might get fired. But he was sticking with it until he got enough money to pay the minimum fare to buy passage to Europe, and that was it. That was the entire plan."

On December 7, 1954, Chuck and Emmett set sail, tourist class, aboard the SS Italia, bound for Southampton, England. As the ship pulled out of New York harbour and sailed past the Statue of Liberty, Emmett noticed a young woman leaning on the ship's railing. She was in tears. Emmett approached her and said, "Whoever he is, he's not worth it." Later he would learn that, in fact, she had just left her boyfriend standing on the docks and she knew she would never see him again. Emmett and the young German woman, Jutta Schick, spent the rest of the week's voyage dancing, eating fine food, and enjoying each other's company to the exclusion of all others. Jutta lived in the small German town of Neumunster, between Hamburg and the Danish border. As 'luck' would have it, Emmett managed to pass through Neumunster several times and the two continued their relationship. In Emmett's words, "We began to fall in love."

"When we got to Europe, Emmett went up to Hamburg," says Chuck. "I didn't know why he was going up there so much, but obviously it was her. He wasn't interested in Europe anymore – he was interested in her!"

Emmett didn't spend all of his time in Hamburg. He travelled throughout Europe and the British Isles, hitchhiking, backpacking and staying in youth hostels. Before he left, he had arranged to send regular reports to the *Canoga Park News,* describing his trip and giving interpretations of Europe through the eyes of an eighteen year old. He wrote of the run-in with the police in Scotland, playing harmonica and singing American folk songs in Ireland, about the rain in France, the beauty of Swiss Alps, hitchhiking along the Riviera into Italy, living the high life in Vienna for $1.87 per day. He wrote about the "large, modern buildings in the city side by side with ruined structures bombed during the war" in Germany and the different versions of English he heard on his trip. According to the young Emmett, New Zealanders spoke the most like Americans and Scotsmen, who "are scarcely understandable in their own land to an American", the least. Emmett's columns wrapped up with the young traveler writing from a little town near Copenhagen, where he compared the countries of Europe to families living on a typical suburban street. He did a commendable job describing the conflict and concord between the countries and likening their cultural personalities to the neighbours you would find living next door to each other. "Germany doesn't get along with Mr. and Mrs. France, Mrs. France finds the Hollanders very dull, the Italians get along with everybody. The Austrians think Mr. Germany works much too hard and takes life too seriously. Finally there's a special feud between Mr. Ireland and Mr. and Mrs. England; this feud is also about past grudges," writes Emmett, "but what makes it worse is that Mr. Ireland must work at the firm Mr. England happens to be owner of, so old Ireland goes to work every day with a chip on his shoulder. He must take what Mr. England has to offer, whether he likes it or not..." Pretty insightful observations for an eighteen year-old.

"Emmett was an independent guy," says Hunt. "Throughout the trip we would split and he would go one way, I'd go the other. Then we'd regroup. Emmett wasn't the following type. He thought individually. When he wanted to go in a direction, he'd figure out how to do it and go. That's a good trait. I don't remember any arguments. He was an easygoing, but independent travelling companion.

"I had written letters back to folks too and they were published in a Valley newspaper," Chuck continues. "When I got home, Emmett had taken all my letters and either typed them up or had them typed up. He painted the front of a three-ring binder, put all my letters in there and gave it to me. That was a great welcome home gift. I still have that and was always grateful that he did that."

After Emmett returned to the States, he and Jutta sent letters back and forth for about a year. It was soon clear to both that they belonged together and plans for a reunion quickly took shape. In February 1956, in Vancouver, British Columbia, Canada, that reunion took place. On June 9, 1956, Emmett and Jutta were married at a Pentecostal Four Square Church in Vancouver.

While in Vancouver, Emmett enrolled in classes at the University of British Columbia and worked as a journeyman reporter for the *Vancouver Sun* newspaper. Their time in Canada was short-lived however, and soon after the wedding the Chapmans moved back to California. They borrowed $300 from Emmett's brother Jerry, $300 from their real estate agent and bought a new $12,000 home in an Encino Park tract housing development. "This was a time when opportunities for young Americans were still plentiful," says Emmett. The new family settled into life in Southern California and on November 3, 1957, Jutta gave birth to their first child: a daughter they named Diana.

Emmett continued his college education and enrolled in UCLA. He graduated with a bachelor's degree in political science. To support the family Emmett worked nights operating a drill press, drilling holes into aircraft and missile parts at Bendix Aviation, where his dad Laverne worked. Yuta (now Yuta, rather than Jutta, because she was frustrated with people mispronouncing her name in English) did office work during the days. For his first two years at UCLA, Emmett studied full-time and held down a full-time job in the evenings.

The Chapmans were a typical young family, facing the struggles all young families face: putting food on the table, trying to get ahead in life and maintaining a husband/wife relationship with a very young child in the picture. Added to all of this was Emmett's growing love of playing music. The workload was gruelling. Emmett followed Laverne's work ethic and kept busy, moving in all sorts of directions simultaneously. Then, in his senior year at UCLA, Emmett had an idea. He calls it his "Big Idea," the way to free himself from the backbreaking, mind-numbing drill press operator job.

Years earlier, Emmett had bought himself a ukulele so he could accompany himself when he sang. By 1959, a guitar had replaced Emmett's ukulele and he was playing and singing the standards of the day. He imitated Johnny Mathis's smooth, rich sound on tunes like "Misty" and "Chances Are." While Emmett claims that he approached his music at the time only as a hobby, as with his other hobbies, he approached music full force. He went so far as to have some of his original songs professionally recorded. Then inspiration struck. "I'd been practicing guitar and singing," he says, "and I decided that I needed to put together a band: a trio with piano, guitar and drums. I'd play guitar, but I'd also function like the bass player in the band. So that's what I did."

(A full-fledged jazz guitarist.)

Like his mother on Rush Street in Chicago, albeit less flamboyantly, Emmett hit the clubs along Ventura Boulevard and had little difficulty landing gigs. At his mother's insistence, he dropped the 'Chapman' and christened his group "The Emmett Howard Trio." The band revolved around Emmett and seven or eight other musicians who would rotate through whenever they were available. The other musicians were eager for the work and marvelled at how easily Emmett seemed to be able to get jobs. His last year at UCLA, he dropped the drill press altogether and worked his way through school playing eight gigs a week and making enough money to support his family.

(The Emmett Howard Trio at Rand's.)

On September 13, 1960, Emmett signed a three-month contract with Ray C. Rand, owner of Rand's Round Up, a chain of six restaurants located throughout Los Angeles. The restaurants were open from 4 p.m. to 2 a.m. nightly. A prime rib dinner cost 79 cents and two could have the "Famous Chuck Wagon Meal" for only $2.95. The contract stipulated that three musicians, including the leader

(Emmett) would work for "4 ½ hours per day for six days each week[7], at a rate of $35.00 per day for the services of all three musicians, including the leader." Emmett had the right to "replace either or both side men but all three musicians [had to] be properly qualified and rehearsed before playing." Rand's had "the option to engage The Emmett Howard Trio including the leader, for an additional three months at a rate of $40.00 per day worked." Emmett, Rand, Ronald F. Rose and Theodre A. Rissi signed the contract.

The Emmett Howard Trio thrust Emmett into the thriving Los Angeles jazz scene of the late fifties and early sixties. Taking their lead from New York and Miles Davis, emerging cool jazz players like Chet Baker and Gerry Mulligan drew people's ears and eyes to the West Coast. Shelly's Manne Hole was a regular stop for the big players of the day, as was The Lighthouse in Hermosa Beach. Jazz spread down from these heights to the smaller clubs and halls throughout Southern California. This was still the age of the small group with the hot soloist, but on the West Coast, the soloists had become a little more introspective.

With ears wide open, Emmett was drawn in two directions: first of all, to jazz guitar players. Three played pivotal and influential roles. All three, in Emmett's words, "explored the orchestral possibilities of the instrument." Perhaps George Van Eps best exemplifies these possibilities.

Van Eps was a pioneering seven-string guitar player. Some seven-string guitarists add a higher string on the top end of the instrument; some add one to the lower end. Van Eps exploited this extended range and extended room by adding a lower string, tuned to an A (a fifth below the regular lowest guitar string's E) and providing

---

[7] Daily, twice on Sunday (afternoon and evening shows), Mondays were a night off.

chordal accompaniment to his melodic lines. During the late fifties and early sixties, Van Eps made a series of solo recordings that pushed the envelope and fully exposed the extended compositional range of his playing and the extended sonic range of his instrument.

Tal Farlow played with a more bare bones approach: fast, creative lead lines and counterpoint. Farlow is famous for filling up a room with his driving rhythms, lightning speed, innovative style and unique sense of harmony. Like most jazz guitarists, Farlow played as a sideman with countless bandleaders; however, it was the albums he recorded with his own group, *Tal*, *This is Tal Farlow*, and *The Tal Farlow Album* that secured his place as one of the preeminent jazz guitarists of his generation.

Barney Kessel was Emmett's third guitar inspiration. Kessel's *Poll Winners* trio consisted of the uncommon combination of bass, drums and guitar. It was almost unheard of at the time, to have a small group with such bare bones instrumentation. Emmett couldn't imagine that these three instruments alone could provide a full enough sound to be interesting. Yet Kessel on guitar, Ray Brown on bass and Shelly Manne on drums pulled it off with style, flair, passion and excitement[8].

Jazz pianists caught Emmett's ears next: notably Oscar Peterson and McCoy Tyner. These players offered the jazz world new chord voicings and sounds, along with new interpretations of rhythm and harmony. Drawing on classical music and music from other cultures, they revolutionized the popular jazz world.

---

[8] Kessel, Brown and Manne had won polls in *Down Beat*, *Playboy* and *Metronome* Magazines in 1956, hence the name of the group, and the inspiration for these three heavyweights to join forces and record their first *Poll Winners* album in 1957. The group recorded four albums, and then disbanded in 1960. In 1975, they reformed and recorded their fifth and final album together.

As a guitarist with The Emmett Howard Trio, Emmett often found himself playing the role of both guitarist and bassist. He turned the bass tone up, emphasizing the lower sonic spectrum and supported the piano player's solos with single note bass lines. He describes his sound as "a bass with chords." The guitar offers the potential to play both chords and melody simultaneously. Guitar, piano, harp, vibraphone – any instrument that plays more than one note at a time – offers the player polyphony, the ability to play more than one note at the same time. Yet even on these polyphonic instruments, with the exception of the piano, most people approach them either as melodic instruments and play one note at a time or as harmonic instruments and play chords. From the beginning of his guitar career, Emmett strove to do both, and play chords and melody at the same time. He could do it on accordion, so why couldn't he do it on guitar?

Emmett had grown musically into what he calls "a full-fledged jazz guitarist." He had successfully turned his solo guitar playing and singing into a trio with him on guitar and vocals, a pianist and drummer. The Emmett Howard Trio found enough work so that he was able to leave the drill press behind. Not surprisingly, he considered music to be a vacation compared to Bendix Aviation, and jumped when the opportunity to play music offered itself. Music had saved the day. With Yuta doing office work and Emmett playing in the evenings, the Chapmans managed to make ends meet.

Emmett graduated from UCLA in 1961 with plans of joining the U.S. Foreign Service. He took the entrance exam and needed to score in the high 90th percentile to get in. He didn't make it. But where one door closes, another one opens and even though the Foreign Service may not have had a place for him, the LA jazz scene did. Emmett became a full-time jazz guitarist.

Later in 1961, Emmett, Yuta and daughter Diana traveled to Germany to visit Yuta's homeland. Emmett brought his guitar. By then, he had already begun making alterations to his instrument. He claims that the thought of leaving his guitar unaltered never entered his mind. Modifying, altering, refining his guitar was "as natural as changing hobbies in childhood." Emmett had a sound in his head and possessed the inquisitiveness and incentive to try and create that sound.

Emmett became a minor celebrity in Germany. He was known as "The American Guitarist in Hamburg with the Weird Guitar." His guitar was a solid body National with a standard body shape, but he placed a cut-down toy block (on loan from Diana) behind the nut at the low end of the guitar's neck, thus extending the instrument's range. He also added springs underneath the bridge and suspended tailpiece. This produced a vibrato and pitch bend effect when manipulated with his right palm. The local jazz musicians were impressed. The public at large, however, did not seem to take too much interest in the American with the weird guitar. Emmett played at a club on Schmuckstrasse, four doors down from a club called *Kaiserkeller*. At the same time, rock and roll played by four young lads from Liverpool was all the rage at *Kaiserkeller* and attracting the lion's share of attention from the Hamburg music community.

On December 27, 1962, while still in Hamburg, Emmett and Yuta's second daughter, Grace[9] was born. Shortly thereafter, the Chapmans moved back to the States and Emmett once again re-invented himself.

---

[9] Inadvertently named after Grazia Lorette, "The Terror of the Village."

By 1962, when Emmett, Yuta and their two daughters left Europe, change was already in the air. Both the post war boom and idealism of the 50s were quickly morphing into two diametrically opposed forces, destined to collide. The Cuban Missile Crisis had heightened global Cold War tensions and the US was firmly committing itself to the conflict in Vietnam. On the entirely opposite side of the fence, the young baby boomer generation was quickly becoming a force and would soon, by sheer numbers, threaten to overtake the status quo. Emmett straddled both worlds. On the music front, Elvis Presley ruled the charts. Over in England, the Beatles were struggling to be signed by a major recording label and a group called the Rolling Stones had just formed.

In September 1963, just before his twenty-seventh birthday, with the family growing and feeling the mounting pressures to support his wife and two daughters, Emmett enlisted in the Air Force. His first assignment was officer training school at Lackland Air Force Base, near San Antonio, Texas. Lackland Air Force Base was tagged "The Gateway to the Air Force." In addition to training enlisted men, Lackland's Officer Training School (OTS) commissioned college graduates who, like Emmett, had no prior military service. With the country preparing for an impending conflict, the base would swell to the size of a small city. Routinely, Lackland would handle more than 20,000 recruits at any given time.

Emmett says, "It was traditional Air Force basic training. Even more rigorous maybe, not just physically but morally and mentally challenging as well. A very, very tough environment to be in."

But even to this tough environment Emmett brought his guitar. Although, during the entire three months he was there, it never made it out of the basement of his barracks.

On November 22, 1963 at 12:30 pm, when John F. Kennedy was shot in Dallas, Texas, Emmett was also in Texas. He was on the parade ground at Lackland. "There was a collective sigh," he remembers. "A stunned exhale, and then just a few seconds later the military band struck up "Dixie." I've never been able to figure out why. Nobody ever commented on it but it seemed totally out of place."

Charged times indeed.

From Lackland, Emmett was sent to Lowery Air Force Base in Denver, Colorado for an eight-month photo-intelligence training program. With the intensity of officer basic training behind him, Emmett's guitar made its way out of the basement and back into his hands. In Denver he had a regular gig with Ed Bacinich, a well-known Greek bouzouki player. Bacinich is best known for playing with the Banat Tamburitza Orchestra[10]. He introduced Emmett to odd rhythms, the importance of groove, and exotic sounds. "Everybody liked my interpretation of the odd rhythms," Emmett said, "even the belly dancers at the club." The club they played at was a popular Denver nightspot. Emmett remembers big name jazz players performing there when they were in town.

Emmett was playing a seven-string guitar custom made by Mark Geiger, the son of the famous violin maker Leroy F. Geiger. Unlike Van Eps, who added a lower string, Emmett added a seventh string that was tuned a fourth higher than standard guitar tuning, extending

---

[10] The tamburitza is a family of plucked-string instruments from the Pannonian region of Southeast Europe.

the range of the instrument higher in pitch. Emmett cut down .007 inch piano wire and wrapped a ball end around the end of the string to affix it to the bridge unit. The guitar's bridge had a lever built into it that he could pop into place, thus raising or lowering the pitch of all the strings. "It wasn't meant for vibratos. It just went 'clunk' and jumped every string to the next pitch," he says. Often, the exceptionally thin first string would break. His theory was that during performances he would be able to play equally well in all keys, without having to adjust his hand positions. While the note pitches moved up and back down a half step, the relationship of the notes to the position markers on the instrument would remain unchanged. His hands would play in comfortable positions, but the sound would match up with more difficult keys. The pitch of the open strings would change too, but Emmett didn't make much use of the open strings. Like many other traditional jazz guitarists, his technique gravitated towards moving chords, scale shapes and patterns around the instrument's fretboard.

After training in Denver, the Chapmans moved to Omaha, Nebraska, where Emmett went to work interpreting satellite photography at the Strategic Air Command (SAC) headquarters. This was the major command center for the Air Force, with housing for over 2,000 families, its own hospital, commissary and library. The big B-52 planes and all the top pilots flew out of the base.

Wife and daughters all wholeheartedly supported Emmett's Air Force career. Yuta was very happy to be an Air Force wife. She was glad for the stability and the respectable position Emmett quickly attained and she was proud to be part of that side of American culture.

"The monthly pay was very low for officers though," says Emmett, "especially second lieutenants, which was my rank at the time. But we had low-priced food from a very well stocked commissary, free medical services and we simply made do. Things were not expensive but we still didn't buy much and our needs were taken care of."

Emmett spent a little over a year and a half working at SAC headquarters. His four-year enlistment was at the halfway point when he was sent to Vietnam, for a four-month tour. Emmett, along with a group of other officers, commanded a Strategic Air Re-locatable Photographic Facility or SARPF unit. This unit consisted of a dozen trailers that could be air-lifted, relocated and then accordion-pleated together to make a sealed, secure and clean environment for photo developing and interpretation. Emmett's SARPF was based out of Tonsinute Air Force Base in Saigon. As with his stint at Lackland, music accompanied Emmett to Vietnam. This time, two amplifiers and the seven string Geiger guitar made the journey.

"My colonel was *very* disapproving when he saw me hauling those off the back of a flatbed truck," said Emmett. He blasted Emmett, insisting that no one could bring such things to Vietnam. But there wasn't much that could be done; they were already in country. However, even though the intention to play was there, just like at Lackland, the guitar stayed in its case for the entire four-month deployment.

From Vietnam, he was sent back to Nebraska and back into the labyrinthine depths of the SAC headquarters' photographic interpretation community. Emmett learned a lot in his last year in the Air Force. He was gaining ground, establishing himself with his peers and doing a lot of overlapping work with other departments. He began learning other uses for the photography, beyond interpretation, including deployment strategies and more advanced military tactics.

"It was getting interesting," he says. "But I was getting more and more interested in becoming a musician and moving back to LA." In November 1967, after completing his four-year commitment and achieving the rank of captain, Emmett left the Air Force with plans to head back to Los Angeles.

While in the Air Force, music was Emmett's constant: a creative escape that he could access and pursue regardless of whatever else he was doing. The April 5, 1965 *Omaha Sun* newspaper featured a story of an Air Force jam session. "Complete freedom to express the art they love," reads the article, complete with a picture of "Lt. Emmett Chapman... commanding his guitar."

Emmett was also continually experimenting with his instrument. He modified and tinkered with it, searching for different ways to control, to change, to make both the sound from the guitar and the way in which sound was created by the guitar unique. He says his experimenting with the guitar itself was unhindered by a formal musical education, and fostered by an analytical, scientific mind that was naturally attracted to systems and logical order. To that, one could add a sense of humour and curiosity. Emmett calls it a "sense of taking the ridiculous to the extreme" to see if there's something useful there. Regardless, all of the modifications Emmett made on his instruments served a purpose. Each change moved him closer and closer to the sounds in his head. "Humour marks the moment when our ego regains some territory from oppressive conscience," wrote Erik Erikson in *Young Man Luther*. Humour acts as a way to work around and to circumvent the tendencies of a character that is naturally drawn to order. It acts as the necessary counterbalance to structure and order, two sides of a greater whole. This is not a conscious act; rather it's a reflection of heredity and environment.

Emmett was enamoured with chords and enamoured with improving his guitars. In one sense, he was trying to realize the extended chords, range and harmony of Van Eps and the influential piano players. In another sense, and perhaps more importantly, Emmett was trying to create his own reality on the guitar. He was trying to forge his own, unique way to both control and create his own musical presence.

On a standard tuned guitar, the interval – the difference in pitch – between the second and third strings is different from the intervals between every other string. This interval, in musical terms, is called a major third. The other intervals are called perfect fourths. On Emmett's guitars, this major third interval moved lower and lower: first, between the third and fourth strings, then the fourth and fifth and eventually right off the instrument. The result was a guitar tuned entirely in perfect fourths. Bass guitars, cellos, violins, mandolins and many other stringed instruments commonly use uniform tunings. The intervals between all the strings are the same. On a standard guitar, chord shapes and scales only work in specific places due to the odd interval between the second and third strings. On uniformly tuned instruments, like Emmett's guitar had now become, chords and scales are instantly transferable to any location because the relationship between the strings is constant everywhere on the neck. Emmett's guitar had become logical. In his words, "a logical, blank slate."

He didn't stop there.

Emmett reversed the order of the pitch of the three lowest strings. On a standard guitar, the note names of these three lowest strings are E, A and D. The E is the lowest pitch. Emmett kept the letter names of the strings intact, but altered their pitch. The D was dropped an octave and became the lowest pitch on the instrument. The E was raised an octave. The result was twofold: the range of the guitar had been extended and the guitar now played from the center outward. The lowest strings ran up the interior of the instrument. From this point on, Emmett approached his guitar as two separate instruments on one guitar neck: a bass and chord grouping of strings ascending in perfect fifths from the center of the neck and a melody group ascending in perfect fourths. Both groupings extended outward, rising in pitch from the interior of the fingerboard.

Extra strings were added; most interestingly, a string Emmett calls the "wild string." The wild string ran in unison with the guitar's normal, high-pitched E string and was controlled by an automobile gearshift that acted as a lever attached to the guitar. The string could be dropped an octave lower in pitch, brought back up, stopped and manoeuvred in various ways by using the right elbow to manipulate the gear shift. From there, Emmett turned to altering the way the sound was produced. He experimented with several different picks and ways of setting the strings in motion. This culminated in the use of a modified baby comb, on loan from Grace, which made the guitar sound like a cello.

Emmett was no longer playing the seven string Geiger guitar. Completely from scratch, he'd built his own instrument with all his modifications and altered tunings. He brought his homemade guitar back to Los Angeles with him and found a very different Los Angeles than the one he had left four years earlier. In short order however, his homemade guitar would earn the name The Freedom Guitar.

Chapter 5 – Captain Chapman in Fantastic LA

Once again, I'm at the kitchen table at Stick Enterprises. The old family photos have been put away and replaced with early Stick snapshots: Emmett with Barney Kessel at Shelly's, Emmett solo, Stick #101 raised triumphantly above LA. Brother Dan took these photos.

Emmett has disappeared somewhere, leaving Dan and me alone to wade through the history. Brother Dan has been there since the beginning. Captain Emmett Chapman used to travel from SAC HEADQUARTERS in Omaha, Nebraska to Los Angeles to visit his family and jam with his little brother's band: The Vanilla Rain. Legend has it that at their high school, The Vanilla Rain was more popular than the Beatles. Fred Cory played guitar and had the Jimi Hendrix sound down cold. Youth, freedom, passion, fire - Emmett's window into the young, electric California of 1969.

Dan and I look at the photos and I start asking questions:

Jim Reilly: *So you've been involved in this since pretty much the beginning?*

Dan Chapman: *Pretty much. I watched him make it.*

JR: *And, he was playing with you when the genesis moment happened.*

DC: *That's true. I was with this group and we were the guys who practiced for ten hours a day. I was the lead singer and I played the harmonica. So I practiced on my harmonica ten hours a day, just to be like the other guys. I got pretty good. We all did.*

One guy in the band was a real inspiration to Emmett. He was a great player. He sounded like Hendrix, played like him too, all over the guitar. He actually gave up the guitar, which is really too bad, but that's another story.

JR: *That would be Fred?*

DC: *Right, Fred Cory. He was a really talented player. Emmett wanted to have the kind of flexibility with music that Fred had. That was all around the time that Hendrix was inspiring everybody. So, that's when we started playing some weird music with Emmett.*

Emmett had this little string on his guitar and he had this thing on the bottom of his guitar where he could move his elbow and it stretched the string out. He always had a little bit extra. He was experimenting all the time with different things on the guitar and then it just seemed to evolve into The Stick. The hammer-on technique was what Hendrix was doing too. He would strum one note and then finger it. And so that kind of led Emmett to that feeling, that spark.

JR: *And then the other hand came around and started tapping, which was the big deal, the different thing?*

DC: *Yeah, he was always striving for that. And I think the whole 'Jazz Elitism' that we talked about was really a genesis for him because they wanted pure improvisation. You know, guys like Coltrane just wanted to 'walk the earth.' Just like in* Pulp Fiction, *you remember that? Samuel Jackson, his ambition in life was to just 'walk the earth.' It was sort of like that. You just had your axe and that's all you wanted to do, was just play it freely, like poetry almost.*

So that kind of led to that orchestral independence. You didn't want to have accompaniment, necessarily. You wanted it all to be there, at the touch of a finger. A very purist attitude actually.

JR: *So what songs were you doing? What kind of stuff were you doing as a band?*

DC: Well, at that time we were really into improvisation. So we would invent these blocks of songs and then just go off and play, and jam. We were just a cover band in those days. Then we evolved into semi-serious musicians, jazz and blues influenced, we did a lot of improvisation. And then I got into song writing. I actually wanted to be a pop songwriter. That's kind of where I was at. My friends and I, we seriously wanted to be the Beatles...

Back in Los Angeles, step brothers Ron and Jerry had moved out on their own, leaving only youngest brother Dan at home. Over the years, regardless of the distance, the Chapmans would send audio recordings, like spoken letters, back and forth. Brother Dan says that those recordings reflected the times they were recorded in, and conveyed a sense of innocence, idealism and togetherness. Laverne, Venetia and young Dan had moved up the San Fernando Valley to Grenada Hills and once Emmett's life had moved into a more consistent rhythm at SAC Headquarters, he would often make the trip west to visit.

"It was always a breath of fresh air to hear from him," says Dan. "It was a hard time for me personally. My parents were older than most people's and very religious. My other brothers were gone. I was almost like an only child." On his visits home, and through the audio letters, Emmett encouraged and supported Dan. He gave his younger brother piano lessons, encouraged him to draw and nurtured his artistic side.[11]

Change was in the air, in more ways than one. As the early part of the decade drew closer and closer to the Summer of Love, the youth,

---

[11] Dan would later become a celebrated artist and graphic designer in the Hollywood film industry.

the baby boomers, were poised to take over and Dan was right in the thick of things. "In order to feel hip," he says, "I would get my mom to drive into Hollywood and go down to Hollywood Blvd. It was the only place to buy hound's tooth or plaid pants. Once, I got a gold shirt and a fringe jacket. My friends and I grew our hair out and had headbands and beads – all the styles of the blooming hippie generation."

On the radio, the Beatles had their first number one single in 1963 with "Please Please Me." On the other side of the mountains from Grenada Hills, near the foot of Laurel Canyon, The Whiskey A-Go-Go opened its doors. Around this same time, Dan had relocated to a new high school. His interest in music and technology gave him an in with similar-minded kids at school and before long, he had formed a band with his new high school friends.

TIME OUT from rehearsal is taken by members of Vanilla Rain new rock 'n' roll group consisting of local high school students. From left are Larry Duff, Fred Khoury, Bill Clark, Danny Chapman, kneeling, Dave Dahlquist and Dennis Wilkinson. Five of young men attend Granada Hills High School while sixth goes to William Howard Taft High School. Group has received contract to play at local center. The News photo

(The Vanilla Rain, 1967. Photo courtesy of Dan Chapman)

They called themselves The Vanilla Rain and quickly became the most popular band at school, complete with groupies. Dan sang and played harmonica; Fred Cory (originally Khoury) played lead guitar; Dennis Wilkinson played rhythm guitar and sang harmony vocals; Larry Duff was the organ player; Dave Dahlquist played bass and Bill Clark rounded out the group on drums. Throughout high school they would play cover tunes at dances and parties, but as they grew older, they began writing their own music. By the end of Dan's high school years, as the early sixties became the later sixties and the musical, cultural and spiritual revolution was peaking, The Vanilla Rain dove headfirst into the psychedelic times. Jimi Hendrix, Paul Butterfield and Eric Clapton inspired the young band mates to practice 10 to 12 hours a day, trying to be virtuosos like their heroes.

"Fred went over the top," says Dan. "He was kind of a compulsive guy anyway, but when he decided to play guitar seriously, he took it to the next level." Dan kept singing and practicing harmonica with the same fervour as the rest of the band, and became a pretty good blues harp player. But it was Cory who most excited Emmett.

On trips to visit the family, Emmett often found himself jamming with The Vanilla Rain. "Fred was a great guitarist," says Emmett. "He sounded like Jeff Beck and Jimi Hendrix mixed together. He was a little guy, looked Italian, but was really Lebanese, raised in suburban California. He influenced me in a lot of ways. I listened to him a lot and it changed a lot of what I was doing on the guitar and how I was hearing music."

"I remember playing with Emmett in Danny's rec room in Granada Hills," says Fred. "We jammed a lot. Emmett was right on course with wanting what other people wanted in that generation. He was older but still wanted what the youth had, which was pretty much to be free. We wanted to express ourselves whether it was music or painting on walls or whatever."

Emmett was living in two worlds: Captain Chapman's Air Force, with structure and responsibility and Brother Dan's Los Angeles of change, music, freedom and seemingly endless possibilities. Looking back, Dan questions how much Emmett really liked being in the Air Force. "I think it was more of a financial thing," Dan says, "job security, a safe thing to do and a way to support the family. He complained about Nebraska. He didn't like that it was landlocked and said that the people there were too conservative."

Emmett echoes Dan's thoughts. "I was real a dissident in the Air Force," he says. "I was letting my hair get a little longer. It wasn't hippie long, but it was long by Air Force standards. I started wearing granny glasses. I was philosophically at odds with the war in Vietnam from the beginning. I was reading Walter Lippman's[12] columns about it and so that kind of separated me ideologically from lots of other young Air Force types of my same rank and age. And I was listening to Eric Clapton, Ginger Baker and Jack Bruce in Cream and playing it for some of the officers I worked with. We'd get into pretty heated debates about all these new movements in the mid to late sixties. It was pretty profound then."

For Emmett though, it wasn't a matter of one world versus another. He needed aspects from both worlds. The discipline and intellectual stimulation came from Air Force photo-intelligence. Freedom, passion and fire came from Los Angeles rock and roll.

---

[12] Lippman was an outspoken and influential writer, journalist, and political commentator. He wrote that the Vietnam War was really a civil war amongst the Vietnamese and that the United States shouldn't have gotten involved in it, citing that the French failed anyway and accusing U.S. forces of doing brutal things in the conflict.

The Los Angeles that Emmett returned to bore little resemblance to the Los Angeles he had left in 1963, when he was playing jazz standards at Rand's Round Up. Music, art, pop culture and the hippie generation were now in full swing. Popular music at that time had a sense of spirituality that it never had before. Along with the Beatles came Eastern philosophy. Through music, new ideas flowed into Western culture. Music was the vehicle of change for the baby boomers' coming of age party. It was the peak of the sexual revolution. *Midnight Cowboy,* John Schlesinger's film about a male prostitute's struggles on the streets of New York, became the first (and only) X-rated film to be recognized by the mainstream film industry and win Academy Awards. Sexual, philosophical, political revolution and change were in the air and the young counterculture led the way. The Green movement began. Young university students changed the U.S. involvement in the Vietnam War. The kids were a force to be reckoned with, and music sounded the rallying cry. The music had a spiritual message to it: a message of change and idealism for the world.

On his high school graduation day, Dan remembers sitting outside his school waiting to take the graduating class picture. He could hear bands rehearsing and sound checks going on for the Newport Music Festival at Devonshire Downs in Northridge. The concert was just down the street. Music historians have dubbed Newport the "Woodstock before Woodstock." Jimi Hendrix and Joe Cocker played there and then headed east to Max Yasgur's farm for three days of peace and music. The Byrds, Jethro Tull, Creedence Clearwater Revival, Ike & Tina Turner and Steppenwolf were also on the bill. It was a time of excitement, of people getting together, of young people getting together and feeling like they could change the world. This was what Emmett found when he returned to Los Angeles.

Emmett couldn't claim entrance into Dan's baby boomer generation by birthright. He was too old and in fact, he felt no more connection to that movement than he did to any other movement that had gone before it. He had a regular job, was a family man and had a military haircut but he was drawn, all the same, to the electricity, the energy and the music of the scene.

"I just wanted to be a part of it," says Emmett. "I believed in it, thought it was a powerful change and an advance for human society, a better way that we could collectively behave together. I saw this revolution coming about from the youth generation, simply by sheer numbers. It was very inspiring."

"He was frustrated at seeing this giant revolution taking place with all this wild, crazy colour and people wearing outlandish things," says Dan. "It was a freedom movement and he was sort of buttoned down in his own world of having to pay the bills. He was part of the establishment out of necessity."

Emmett was on the outside of Dan's music scene, but he was practicing with the same drive and passion as Fred, Dan and the rest of their musician friends. He was just as dedicated to becoming a virtuoso on his instrument. Shortly after high school graduation, The Vanilla Rain changed their name to Cotton and devoted themselves to improvising long jams like The Butterfield Blues Band with a bluesier, rock-based style, like Jeff Beck. This fit Emmett's style better and he became a regular part of those jams. But he still hadn't found his voice.

"We were rockers and he was a jazzer," Cory says. "He wanted the kind of musical freedom he heard in John Coltrane's phrasing. He had a concept of musical freedom but he didn't know how to convey it himself."

"He didn't have that abandon yet," says Dan. "He had a lot of knowledge of chords and theory, but in a way, that seemed to get in the way of the abandon. His strict jazz technique was almost too much."

On the last few trips before Emmett moved his family back to LA for good, he'd borrow his parents' car, a Nash Rambler, and go house hunting in the canyon hills around Los Angeles. With money he and Yuta were able to save in the Air Force, he bought a house in Laurel Canyon, on Yucca Trail, for $35,000. His salary had steadily improved and they maintained their minimal expenses. At the time in LA, jobs were hard to come by. After a series of government and private company tests for management type jobs, Emmett landed a job with the California State Civil Service. He worked in the personnel department, interviewing potential employees and doing college recruitment for the personnel board.

Emmett was living a dichotomous life. On one hand was the straight-laced world of interviewing potential civil service auditors, janitors, psychiatric social workers and secretaries. On the other was the wild LA music scene. Just down from his Laurel Canyon home were Sunset Boulevard's hippest clubs: The Roxy and The Whiskey a Go-Go. All kinds of rock musicians and aspiring bands flocked to LA, Hollywood and the hills around the city. Emmett was living in the center of the creative music scene but working as far away from it as one could travel.

"It was beautiful," says Cory, describing the Laurel Canyon scene. "It was a terrific moment in time. It was 1969, *Abbey Road* had just come out and that was the soundtrack of my period there. Emmett was going to his Civil Service job. Yuta was working at an insurance company. Emmett and I would jam. I had my equipment set up at his house, in the daytime, when no one was home and I was able to blast my guitar. I was playing *Are You Experienced* all the time, which also influenced Emmett a lot. I'd keep saying, "you've got to listen to this album." He'd play me John Coltrane, which was his ideal for instrumental phrasing. It was an incredible time for music. Alice Cooper lived down the block, John Mayall lived up the block, Joni Mitchell was there."

(Freddy Cory, early '70s. Photo by Dan Chapman)

"Emmett was stuck in a straight job, but the whole scene in Laurel Canyon was peace and love and hippies. He wanted a part of that. He was coming home with his suit and tie, but the bigger picture was that he wanted freedom. He wanted freedom out of that life. He was seeking freedom musically also, as a way out of being stuck in his nine-to-five life. He liked the whole thing."

"I'd go down to the Roxy and the Whiskey," Emmett says. "Sunset Boulevard was just stacked with people from all over the place – just down at the bottom of the hill. People dressed in weird costumes, flowing gowns, cowboys and Indians, gurus, just everything – every kind of alternative garb you could think of."

"He was dying to be a part of it," Fred continues. "He was right in the middle of that sixties revolution of conformity versus rebellion. He wanted a way out and I guess he chose music as his way out. We would play and I'd be playing at such a volume that I could pick one string and roll my fingers around and tap and get a lot of notes out of just one picking. I think that had some influence on Emmett. He was experimenting with picks, trying to get different sounds that way. Emmett kept coming up with these new shaped picks and I remember having conversations with him, gently kind of saying that he was not a very good picker. He was frustrated picking and that's why he kept inventing so many different picks. In the end, he invented his way out through that limitation. He found a way around his limitations, creatively.

"Our basic conversation as musicians was always about two things: freedom and expression. We talked a lot about it. We talked about how Hendrix was doing stuff that was free and we talked about expression by making the guitar an extension of singing. And emotion too. I think Emmett got a kick out of that trait in me. I was playing on instinct and animalism – which might actually be the same thing – primal stuff, screaming, playing from the aspect of pure emotion. Emmett really got a kick out of that. I don't think that he naturally really is that kind of animal himself."

Emmett's decision to become a fulltime professional musician prompted his move back to LA. Music provided the escape from the graveyard shift at Bendix Aviation and was his passion and much needed creative outlet while serving in the Air Force. Now, he was ready to make it his life's work. The specifics weren't quite clear yet, but the path was presenting itself.

The young, pulsating rock scene was a huge pull for Emmett and he did his fair share of jamming and rehearsing with the overabundance of garage bands around LA. However, he was still firmly rooted in the jazz world. One of Emmett's biggest guitar influences, Barney Kessel, owned and operated a music store in Hollywood. Barney Kessel's Music World, located at 1770 North Vine, on the corner of Vine and Yucca Street, was only in business from 1967 to 1970 but in that short period of time managed to become a beacon for the cream of the crop of West Coast musicians.

Interviewed about his store in 1969, Kessel said, "I have my own shop in Hollywood. It's called Barney Kessel's Music World and it's predominantly a guitar shop. We sell them, we have an excellent repairman and several teachers. I don't teach myself; I give what I call 'consultations,' which is speaking with people at one or two meetings, to direct them as best I can towards what their goals are. Kind of vocational guidance, in a way, with regard to the guitar."

Players of all ages would congregate at Music World, take lessons there and network. John Lennon, George Harrison and Eric Clapton were said to have been customers.

Music World was located on the ground floor of the famous Capital Records building, making it even more of a mecca to serious, aspiring musicians. Being a longtime fan of Kessel, Emmett needed little prompting to check out the shop in the building that looked like a stack of records. Kessel took an immediate liking to him. "I'd go in and show him my latest stuff on guitar, the wild string, the baby comb picks. He was always encouraging and enthusiastic," says Emmett. Kessel recorded some of Emmett's wild string guitar tunes. "We went into his studio and I recorded two of my compositions with his bass player and drummer. They were exotic jazz tunes. They sounded like jazz, but a stranger kind of jazz – exotic and sensuous sounding."

Kessel was receptive to and supportive of Emmett's desire to carve out a musical career. In a letter dated October 20th, 1968, he wrote:

Dear Emmett,

Thank you so much for the beautiful LP. It was very thoughtful and I do appreciate your kindness.

I had to leave without being able to contact you, for which I am sorry, however, you were on my mind.

An opportunity to speak of your merits and qualifications arose recently when a gentleman from Rickenbacker contacted me. I hope this developed into something meaningful and worthwhile for you.

The additional work I had done on your tapes away from Criterion Music led to an unfortunate delay because of a lack of understanding. The work was done and then the company in a desire to be helpful volunteered to deliver the work to my store.

I kept asking at the store if anything had been received but I was told no – it seemed lost – then one day before I left it was found at the store – mistakenly filed away and forgotten – by our well-intentioned and usually efficient assistant.

Lack of time at that point in my schedule didn't allow me to hear the results, nor contact you nor act further on the project. I will return Nov. 5 and will continue at that time, since I have all the pertinent materials in my home.

I hope all is well with you and your nice family. Please say hello to them for me and I will contact you on my return.

Your friend,

Barney

Two worlds had collided. Southern California was the epicenter and Emmett was living simultaneously in both. But neither of those two worlds was home. Belonging to or identifying with any one specific group, political party or ideology never motivated him. Brother Dan's rock band may have been Emmett's ticket into the sixties eclectic counterculture, but he never intended to become a full-fledged member of that club.

"It was never that I wanted to be 'in,'" Emmett says. "I've always felt alienated from everything. It started with religion. It probably started with my parents and not really having a relationship with my biological father. I was always, from childhood, very sceptical of society and didn't like what I saw."

Rather than hitching his horses to one wagon, Emmett took the best of both worlds and created his own set of rules. "As I look back," he says, "I was always trying to be objective in a different way, making a picture of an alternative world by force of imagination."

The dynamics of the sixties and the metaphorical fire of the place, made searching and changing virtually inevitable. For Emmett, change had always been the constant, so nothing was new there. In many respects, the society's uncertainty and flux had actually caught up with Emmett's habitual tendency to embrace those two forces. All these factors were leading up to a moment when the technique and instrument would evolve in an explosive instant. All those forces could only have happened in that one place, that one time and through this one individual.

Culture, music, traditions change. Ironically, it wasn't changing the guitar that would lead to the musical freedom Emmett sought. Extra strings and odd picks all changed the guitar's sound and range. Super-sensitive electric pickups played a critical role. Technology could now meet and facilitate passion. But a radically new technique for playing the guitar, made possible only as a result of all that was around at the time coming together, opened the door for Emmett. Once that door was open, only a new instrument could make the technique viable. Technique first, then the tool.

Nineteen sixty-nine was an apex when young American society was trying to change. Emmett was on top of that: an embodiment of idealism, an instrument of freedom, and freedom of expression. Form, function, tradition and discipline on one hand. Freedom, expression, autonomy and independence on the other. The combination of disciplined jazz and the freedom of Hendrix: innocence and potential.

"That was me," says Emmett. "That has to do with the discovery of the technique. You could do that. You could play a disciplined left hand and a free reeling right hand. You could play snaky legato lines like a rock and roll musician does with the right hand, while you're accompanying yourself in a more orchestral way, with meaning, in the left hand. That's the superiority of western music, going way back to old Italian opera and beyond. Its claim to superiority is that you create a harmonic context for the melody lines, not just an expression of the scale. The scale is nice and sensuous and you can have many of them. They're full of variety and nuance and expression for every occasion, from funerals to weddings, but as soon as you introduce harmony as the background to the melody, it creates meaning."

That quest, that combination of depth and meaning had been Emmett's grail since he was 14 and re-harmonizing all the church hymns on his accordion.

"I saw myself as a chord collector," he says. Even when he was modifying his guitars, he was trying to access the power of chords. "It was the common element to be able to play all these chords and progressions of chords, while at the same time playing melody. That's why I liked George Van Eps so much. That's why I liked Barney Kessel who did the same type of thing as Van Eps but differently. Kessel parceled the vamps between the lines so it was distributed in time, whereas Van Eps played a more vertical concept – inner moving voices, maybe even a more intelligent approach than Barney's gutsier, more visceral approach. Both were doing the same thing: expanding the orchestral capability of the guitar and that's what I wanted to do, while maintaining the freewheeling melody."

On August 26th, 1969, that's exactly what Emmett Chapman did.

Chapter 6 – The Moment of Tap – "It Felt Like Flying"

Jim Reilly (via email): It's almost time to talk again! I've almost finished up to 1969. Having a bit of a struggle creating the two worlds, SAC Headquarters - LA Hippiedome, and how you fit into neither, yet both, at the same time – but it's taking shape. That's actually mirrored in your music: left hand structured and disciplined, right hand free and searching.

Emmett Chapman (reply): Nice one! Engineering together with art. Analysis with synthesis. Order with abandon. Saturn square Jupiter in a sharply focused T-square. That's my game and you tagged it. Gotta have it all.

JR: Now I'd like to focus really in-depth on the moment of tap – explore how in that instant everything fell into place.

EC: The above dichotomy of structure versus freedom, stressful as it is, must find resolution, and when it does, those moments have taken me to the unexpected - something extra, more than the equivalent "bang for the buck" (oomph for the effort)...

IN OTHER WORDS (not via email): On August 26, 1969, everything changed.

Time magazine subtitled their 40th anniversary issue of the events in 1969, "Woodstock, the Moon and Manson: The Turbulent End of the '60s." That Turbulent End to the sixties began with Richard Nixon's swearing in as the 37th President of the United States, 537,500 US troops stationed in Southeast Asia and thousands of protesters opposing the Vietnam War just as fervently at home. On July 20th, Neil Armstrong and Buzz Aldrin walked on the moon. Back on earth a few weeks later, nearly half a million hippies walked on Max Yasgur's farm near Woodstock, NY, for "Three days of Peace and Music." From the hills around Los Angeles, Charles Manson and his cult terrorized the city.

The music world in 1969 was a tale of extremes too, with Woodstock's peace and music at one end, and Altamont's Rolling Stone concert decaying into chaos and murder at the other. One signalled the height of the love generation, the other its end. John Lennon married Yoko Ono in 1969. Elvis returned to the concert stage. The Jackson Five, Led Zeppelin and King Crimson all released their first albums.

For Emmett, on August 26th, 1969, his entire life literally changed. More specifically, the spark, the fire, the force that would enrich, shape and guide his life presented itself. In 1969, Emmett was thirty-two and earning a living working for the California Civil Service. His guitar had extra strings, a longer neck than a regular guitar and an odd, spoon-shaped body. This was the guitar Emmett built in 1965 at SAC headquarters in Omaha, Nebraska. This was "The Freedom Guitar." The Freedom Guitar had evolved into a nine-stringed instrument: the lowest notes in the middle, and the higher notes going out in either direction from the centre of the neck. Emmett was jamming with his brother Dan and his friends. Fred Cory was playing with all the effects, a big Fender amplifier with vibrato and spring reverb and sounding, even looking like Hendrix, when he played.

Emmett had found the sound he wanted. He wanted to play lead melody lines like Hendrix. But, he also wanted to play all the altered, extended chords, inspired by jazz pianists that the Freedom Guitar, with its altered tuning, longer neck and extra strings made possible.

This was the sound in Emmett's head: the power and visceral intensity of rock and roll merged with the intellectual sophistication of jazz.

"Hendrix could make the guitar sing," he says. "Others could as well, like Eric Clapton for example, but no one did it with the *grace and balance* of Hendrix." Emmett wanted that freedom, that grace, balance, self-expression, creativity and abandon.

In the weeks leading up to Emmett's watershed moment, he did a couple of things. First, he resolved only to play standing up. Until this point, he had always played sitting down. While sitting, he observed very specific methods of holding his hands while picking. He insisted on keeping the little finger of his right hand firmly planted on the guitar's body.

"I thought I was comfortable, but I had a very rigid way of picking. I was also discovering guitarists who, for the first time, were picking up on every upbeat and down on every downbeat instead of rolling their picks across strings. Some guitarists ended up being shredders, playing really fast, but on single strings. What these new guitarists, John McLaughlin, Allan Holdsworth were doing was amazing, because they could play so fast. I was getting to a place where I would have learned that technique and thrown the other techniques away, except I started tapping instead."

Second, he oiled his fingerboard so that his fingers could slide freely. For a couple of weeks he practiced playing as fast as he could, standing up and running through scales and chords up and down the neck of his guitar.

"The guitar was becoming like a toy in my hand," Emmett says. "I could play very fast and I could bend the notes and then I started doing what Jimi Hendrix did. Not just picking every note, but picking one note and fingering a whole lot of other notes, and peeling off and hammering-on."

On August 26, 1969 at about 6:30 p.m., Emmett was practicing in his studio, which doubled as the master bedroom of his Yucca Trail home in Laurel Canyon. That instant – and it was merely an instant – was both the end of an old story and the beginning of a new one. In one sense Emmett was at the end of a journey. In another, he was about to embark on a whole new adventure. He suddenly realized how to make the music he heard in his head and felt in his heart. Even though the guitar modifications had taken him close, adding gears, levers and extra strings hadn't uncovered his sound.

In that one instant two things happened. Emmett's right hand, previously confined to its supporting role of picking the strings in a conventional way, moved onto the neck and began tapping the strings. Emmett then shifted the angle of the Freedom Guitar from its normal horizontal position, to a more vertical one. In less than a second, his guitar changed from a traditional horizontally held instrument to a vertically held one. His right hand moved up the neck and Emmett tapped with both hands. Both hands were tapping on the strings with all eight fingers at right angles to the guitar neck and the hands were approaching the fretboard from opposite sides: parallel two-handed tapping.

"It felt like flying," said Emmett.

Both the left and the right hands were flying. His left hand could still play his unique chord voicings, while Emmett's right hand, liberated from its supporting role of setting the strings in motion, could play chords and melody too. He was immediately able to engage both hands in their new roles. "That was the moment for me," he says. "It was a revelation that just said to me: throw all of this, all of those years of guitar playing away and start over again."

Emmett could now access piano players' chords and he could play snaky, fast, intricate melody at the same time. He could do all this on his modified electric guitar that could sound like Hendrix with the distortion, wah-wah, echo and other effects. Emmett was fast, fluent and articulate from the outset.

"I wanted to have a unique guitar voice and I wanted to play orchestrally and I wanted to play freewheeling melodies. That's almost impossible with only one fingering hand, and that's where the other hand came into play. Suddenly I had a very large 'hand' and double the mind and I could do it. It was like a total change of character."

The first sensation was a thrill. The thrill was immediately followed by the realization of an obligation. An obligation to fully explore what he had just discovered. Until that moment, music had been Emmett's hobby. Now, his life's work lay before him.

"I can't remember if he said Eureka! Or Yee Haw!" says daughter Diana. "But he yelled something." She was 12 years old and at home when her Dad discovered his two-handed tapping technique. "I do remember running to his room to see if something was wrong. He's *never* been the kind of person to scream out like that, so I knew something was up."

One story was complete. The hero had found his sound. The next story though, had just been born. Emmett was presented with the germ of his life's quest. Immediately he recognized this and immediately he committed himself to it.

"I don't remember what I yelled," Emmett says. "But I do remember leaping around the house. I remember exactly where I was standing when I came up with the idea, where I was in relation to my recording gear and sound gear."

"It was a moment of resolution and excitement because I recognized immediately that there were extras involved. There were things that went beyond my imagination that just hit me. One of them was to get rid of all the gadgets that I had on my guitar. Another was to play with a very wide, spread out hand. Another was to play independently from the hands. Another was to pluck off, hammer-on/hammer-off, one hand against the other, which made the left hand a very mobile capo[13]. It hit me in a rush that I could do the things that I'd always wanted to do *and* it didn't resemble my old sound at all. My character as a musician completely changed. Not just changing in sound, but a change in music – so it was a total change in character, in personality as a musician. And it was an escape from jazz guitar – it wasn't jazz anymore, it was something else."

Parallel hands tapping with all fingers perpendicular to the strings was a new musical language: a new means of performing. A new means of performing almost invariably creates new music. This is what made Emmett's technique special and unique. "A new performing means, a new technique of playing on strings can change the musical results," says Emmett. "That's what this technique, the Stick technique, had – and I called the technique 'Free Hands.' I named my guitar 'The Freedom Guitar' in 1969 and then I came up with the technique I later called Free Hands. A new instrument can change music."

---

[13] A capo is a device used to permanently hold the strings against the frets of a stringed instrument, thus shortening the string length and raising the pitch of all the strings a set amount.

Emmett's way of tapping his guitar strings, the angle at which he approached the neck of his guitar and the way he held his instrument vertically rather than horizontally, hadn't been done before. Although Emmett was the first known guitarist to line up his hands parallel to the fretboard, he wasn't the first guitar player to tap his guitar strings. For ages, the stringed-instrument musicians' toolbox included hammer-ons and pull-offs. Emmett's influences, Hendrix, John McLaughlin, Jimi Page, Fred Cory, integrated those ornamentations, thereby infusing unparalleled expression into their playing. Tapping on strings as an ornamentation had long been part of the guitar's, violin's and other stringed instruments' repertoires. Two notable guitar players used a two-handed tapping method similar in theory, but not in practice, to Emmett's before Emmett discovered his technique.

Jimmie Webster was a jazz guitarist and innovator who, as early as the 1950s, developed an independent two-handed tapping technique on the electric guitar; however, it was much different than Emmett's. Webster held his guitar conventionally, with the right hand approaching the strings like a standard guitarist. His right arm, hand, and fingers were parallel to the strings and he tapped one or two notes at a time with that hand. Webster was successful. He worked for Gretsch Guitars and represented their line to major music retailers. He also wrote an instructional pamphlet describing his technique.

Dave Bunker went one step further and created a double-neck instrument with two playable fretboards, each tapped with one hand. After seeing Webster perform in the late 1950s, Bunker was inspired by his two-handed tapping. After exploring tapping on his guitar, he created his own instrument, patented in 1958, called the Duo-lectar. The Duo-lectar had two separate fingerboards on one guitar body.

One of the fingerboards was wider than a standard guitar neck and was meant for playing melodies and chords; the other was tuned like a four string bass and meant for bass lines. Bunker's instrument, like Webster's, was held like a traditional guitar.

While both Webster and Bunker created and employed viable techniques, there are a couple of major differences between what they did and what Emmett discovered. Other players tapped with their right hand parallel to the strings. Emmett tapped with both hands perpendicular to the strings approaching the neck from opposite sides. Holding a tapping instrument like a regular guitar (picking hand parallel to the strings) severely limits the possibilities of right-hand techniques. Using one or two fingers to poke or punch individual notes means that the entire right arm must move back and forth to play scales and melodic runs. Without adjusting the angle of the fretboard, the right wrist must bend significantly in order to approach the strings in a way that comfortably accesses a full range of chords. Their discoveries remained virtually unknown to guitarists and teachers, and were not passed on. By shifting the angle to an almost vertical position (hands perpendicular to neck) the strings line up at right angles to the fingers and the notes line up as a sequence along the frets.

With the instrument horizontal, in order to play scales or single note runs, the player must move their entire right arm at the shoulder. This can be done effectively, but lacks practicality. It's cumbersome. What Emmett found was a way for both the right and left hands to stay in a single position along the neck, and access a full range of notes and chords. Both hands were equal partners. This had never been done before. It was a synthesis of all that he had already done and a foreshadowing of all that was to come – a synthesis of guitar, bass, piano, even percussion into one instrument. Emmett had no knowledge of other guitar tappers beyond the Hendrix-type, rock guitar, fret-hand pyrotechnics. Neither Bunker nor Webster had influenced him.

At first, when Emmett was jumping around the house showing everyone his new discovery, the family was interested, but not surprised or overly excited. "He had always been playing around and altering his guitars," says Diana. "At first, it seemed like this was just another one of his many, many new ideas."

Emmett agrees, "Yes, they took it for granted. I was a jazz guitarist after all. How inspiring is that to a family?"

Other musicians' reactions were immediate. "I could play right away," says Emmett. "I could play songs and I performed right away. Just from one day to the next, I could improvise and then I would start to work on songs. "Yesterday" and "A Whiter Shade of Pale" were among the first. The technique was the invention, and it happened on a guitar, so I took a couple of days, put a damper on my guitar, brought the action down even lower than it was, quit using my very thin picks and baby comb picks and explored two-handed tapping."

Emmett's first stop with The Freedom Guitar and two-handed tapping was Fred and brother Dan's band Cotton. Emmett eagerly took his newly expanded range, expanded technique, and expanded rhythmic, harmonic and melodic possibilities, and went to jam with the band. Right away, it was clear that this was a new Emmett, no longer filling his previous role as lead or rhythm guitarist. There was now so much more. His playing was much greater, more all-encompassing. He sounded like a one-man band.

It didn't fit.

"He wasn't a band guy anymore and we were a band," says Fred. "I saw him changing right before my eyes. It was a time of change, of people seeking freedom versus establishment and conformity, for lack of a better cliché. He wanted to express what seemed like a subdued type of personality. The change in Emmett I saw was that of a man that was like millions of other people in the sixties who were looking for what I consider to be freedom. It was peace and love and freedom. One day he was like millions of others searching for it and the next day he found it."

"I think the reason we couldn't play with him was because Emmett was doing everything," Dan adds. "He was going everywhere. He was playing melody and bass and there was no room for a band. How could you play with that? We weren't able to play with that."

Dan was Emmett's route into the fire of rock and roll. That fire and the need to express himself musically, took him to his new, independent two-handed tapping technique. Once the technique arrived he didn't need Cotton anymore. Their role in the story had been fulfilled. Dan agrees. "We were the cocoon," he says. Cotton was the final piece, the excuse to be free and radical, to be experimental and open to the muse.

Emmett had played to his strengths. The corporate world and the free-flowing music community had coalesced. He was young enough to embrace and see the potential in the hippie movement, yet old enough to see through the superficial trappings and act upon his creative intuition. The entire moment was only a flash. One instant there was nothing, then a shift, and then nothing could be the same again.

"Sometimes such experiences are just nonverbal," says Emmett. "I was probably too enthused and absorbed to make any detailed notes. Shortly after the discovery though, I did make the briefest note in my ephemeris: "Freedom Guitar!""

Chapter 7 – Would You Welcome Please:
"THE ELECTRIC STICK"

EC: Right, so my goal was to be a musician. I had this Studebaker Gran Turismo V8, beautiful car, and we had this nice house. So what I did was sell the car, buy an old VW with dents in it, paint all the dents a dull black overtop a ladybug-brown, coffee color. So I had a funky old car that ran on hardly any gas at all. Then I built a room down below the main part of the house in the basement. We portioned off a hallway to the two bedrooms, put a hot plate in there and rented that out. Our tenants had the master bedroom; we had the living room, dining room, kitchen and this lower room for Diana and Grace. We did that for three years or so...

Emmett found himself in 1969 with a vision and both the desire and duty to fulfill that vision. He was 33 years old. He had tapped. He had turned his guitar from its traditional horizontal position to a more vertical one, and tapped the strings against the frets with both hands. The decision had been made to embrace music—his music—with full force. He had found a way to create the sound he heard in his head and he didn't look back.

"By that time, we had kind of dug in at home," Emmett says. "I divided the house off so that we could rent out part of it. I quit my Civil Service job with the State of California, sold my gas-guzzling Studebaker Gran Turismo and bought an old VW and just sort of dug in and started to focus on the music.

"As a bonus, I was home and involved with both daughters and other things around the house like cooking with Yuta, washing dishes, giving haircuts, teaching Grace how to read and doing strange artistic things to the house.

"I never liked working a nine-to-five job, ever. The closest I came was that last year when I really got involved in the photo-reconnaissance work in the Air Force. But I was almost like a clock-watcher, just wishing I wasn't there. I had my own dreams. As far as I'm concerned, those dreams are what make history and what make a community. They're important for our future; otherwise it's just more of the same. It's like what Bruce Cockburn said in his song, "The Trouble with Normal:" "The trouble with normal is it only gets worse" – sung to a military cadence.

"It was great to quit work and try and make it as a musician. Yuta actually made it possible because she was still working for the first two or three years. She worked up until 1975 or '76 at the Occidental Insurance Company."

After the unsuccessful jams with brother Dan's band Cotton, Emmett took The Freedom Guitar and his new two-handed tapping technique down to Barney Kessel's Music World.

"I came in [to Kessel's store] one day and I was able to tap with two hands on my instrument. I'd re-worked the setup on my guitar and could play some songs," says Emmett. "He was over the top with enthusiasm. That was just after a couple of months of playing the new technique. Right after that we started rehearsing and we put together a quartet and played around LA." Emmett had gone from being a fan of Kessel's music, to a friend of the man, to a musical collaborator.

Kessel had always been open to new sounds. The electric Los Angeles music scene with the three J's (Janis, Jimi and Jim) holding court, was calling him. The hip scene was all rock and roll, with groups from Love, and the Lovin' Spoonful, to Deep Purple, all playing their parts. As far as the mainstream popular music scene was concerned, jazz was cocktail music and avant-garde jazz was far too sophisticated and cerebral. The LA scene was vital, intense and colourful, but almost exclusively ruled by the rock bands.

Miles Davis had started exploring a rock/jazz hybrid and other jazz players were following suit. This fusion of jazz and rock ignited Kessel's interest, and he wanted a piece of the action. He was looking for a way to add a new energy to his music, to tap into the excitement of the times. Emmett and his newfound sound were just the ticket in.

"I was drumming my fingers with my right hand and playing the chords I already knew with my left hand. I felt comfortable doing that. It wasn't very ambitious compared to what people do on The Stick today, or even what I do on The Stick today, but Kessel thought it was genius. People who heard it back then thought it was of the future."

Kessel asked Emmett to join him; they added a drummer and a bass player, formed The Barney Kessel Cornucopia and debuted at Donte's, in North Hollywood, on April 10, 1970. Approval from Kessel translated into success, acceptance and validation for Emmett's two-handed music.

Cornucopia wasn't your traditional jazz fare. This wasn't the Poll Winner's sound, but that was intentional. Kessel was a traditional jazz player living in a rock and roll world. Emmett says that Barney would often say that he could play better than the famous rock guitarists of the day and he couldn't understand why they were getting all the glory. And while he may have been right, he envied the young hippie rock stars' successes and wanted to enter that world. Cornucopia blurred the lines between rock and jazz and touched on other genres too. It wasn't as heavy as John McLaughlin's Mahavishnu Orchestra but it wasn't old-school jazz either. The initial reviews were encouraging for both Chapman and Kessel:

Daily Variety, *Mon., Apr. 13 1970:*

Donte's – Barney Kessel is still playing the same easy, mellow guitar that has kept him in the top ranks of jazz performers for over a decade. When his set of 11 numbers was caught here he mixed Standards with new tunes, always maintaining the control for which he is noted. Relying on chords to build the tunes rather than a series of single notes, he bridges the chords with lightning-fast single-note runs. He plays a single pickup hollow-bodied Gibson, which accounts for the roundness of the tone he achieves.

He touched all the bases, from Latin to blues to show ballads to a fugue with equal finesse. Standouts were Luis Bonfa's "Manha De Carnival" from the film Black Orpheus, *and "Leftover Dreams"...*

...Emmett Chaplin [sic] on nine-string guitar; Jim Troxel on drums and Ray Neapolitan on bass played the same tight, understated lines Kessel does. Solos were new, but exceptional and Chaplin contributes remarkable rhythm. His versatility and that of the instrument are remarkable.

Change was once again in the air. In the same *Daily Variety,* below Cornucopia's debut review, a small headline reads, "Now Only Three Beatles." A press release from London the day before, officially announced Paul McCartney's split from John, George and Ringo and the release of McCartney's first solo album. Three days later, noted jazz writer Leonard Feather caught Cornucopia at Donte's. Emmett's two-handed tapping technique was only a little more than six months old:

Kessel Four Touches All Bases – Not Tritely

By Leonard Feather

After working in London for almost a year, guitarist Barney Kessel returned a couple of months ago to the Southland, where he recently formed a quartet. Known simply as the Barney Kessel Cornucopia, it is now playing a series of weekends at Donte's.

Having long paid dues as a jazzman, and having learned during his studio years to adjust to every contingency, Kessel might be expected to travel the jazz-rock route that has lured many of his peers. The Cornucopia, fortunately, is as remarkable for what it is not as for what it is.

It is not a sellout or copout combo. Certainly jazz-rock is acknowledged, but only as one view in a panoramic picture that takes in country rock, bossa nova, unhyphenated jazz and as many other idioms as a plectrum can strike.

Web of Strings *– The instrumental makeup of the group enmeshes the listener pleasantly in a web of strings. In "Blue Grass Countryside," for instance, the leader played a 12-string guitar in a contemplative Kentucky-soul conversation with himself, building the momentum slowly with the help of a nine-string guitar invented and played by Emmett Chapman, and the Fender bass of Ray Neapolitan. Total: 25 strings and one lonely unstrung character, Jim Troxel, at the drums.*

That Kessel, in the search for new ground, has not discarded the territorial gains of his illustrious past was illustrated in the cooking jazz on "Old Devil Moon," the blue streak groove of "What Now My Love?," the noble and mobile chording of "Here's That Rainy Day."

Sole Role – *Chapman came to bat in a solo role on "Summertime," emitting all manner of engaging wails and howls.*

Neapolitan is one man who can make the electric bass seem right in just about every context. Troxel occasionally extruded over the guitars, but more often furnished a healthy and heady pulsation.

Kessel intends to keep this unit together, and with good reason. He has a package that could fill a rock palace with gaping-mouth youths, who can learn from him where virtuosic contemporary guitar is really at. The quartet will be making the Friday and Saturday scene at Donte's.

(Emmett and The Freedom Guitar with Barney Kessel at Donte's.)

Cornucopia was working for both musicians. "I'd been looking for this music for a long time," says Emmett. "Barney Kessel was a big inspiration, and in turn, he was inspired by me." Kessel was able to tap into the LA scene's electric currents. Emmett's newfound voice inspired his musical idol. The group played together for about five months. Occasionally Emmett and Barney would play as a duet. In September, they ended up at Shelly's Manne Hole. Leonard Feather was once again in the audience, but his earlier enthusiasm for both Kessel's music and Emmett's playing had cooled:

Music Review, Los Angeles Times, Sept., 1970
Kessel Backed Up by Combo – Leonard Feather

Barney Kessel, whose quartet is at Shelly's Manne Hole this week, has been playing professionally since before most of today's prominent plectrists were born...

In the course of two sets on Tuesday, the music covered so much territory that if Kessel had stopped exploring and sat down in one place and said, "This land is mine," perhaps a clearer group identity would have been established.

Clever Visit *– There was an elaborate and clever visit with "Eleanor Rigby" that began as a fugue, became a waltz, a samba and at last a medium for straight swinging jazz.*

There were great Standards—"Here's That Rainy Day," "Just Friends," "Watch What Happens," all displaying Kessel in optimum form. Completing the repertoire were a funky blues, a rock blues and a couple of unexpected items like "Monday Monday."

Except for a change in bass players (he now has the excellent Jim Hughart on Fender), this is the same combo Kessel introduced some months ago at Donte's, with Emmett Chapman playing a self-invented nine-string guitar and Jim Troxel on drums.

Chapman, who holds the instrument almost vertically, sounded just about as awkward as he looked much of the time. He incorporates all the effects (pseudo-bottleneck, etc.) that are supposedly mandatory in today's guitar world.

For a while, his whining seemed novel and intriguing, but eventually it became merely anticlimactic when his solos followed the leader's. He just didn't seem to belong in the Kessel bag, playing a tune like "The More I See of You," which requires a keen ear for harmonic changes.

Troxel alternated four-beat jazz and lightweight rock. During Kessel's delineation of some of the prettier melodies he upset the mood by supplying a staccato beat where a legato, circular wire-brush motion was called for.

At least 50% of the value of the quartet can be credited to Kessel. True, Chapman's presence, and the use of certain rock disciplines could help blow the mind of a rock audience. But at Shelly's it's the three B's—ballads, bossa nova and blues—that make his formula work best.

It would seem that the group's foray away from Kessel's more accepted traditional jazz voice was wearing thin on the purists. It's interesting that although Feather and other reviewers mentioned Emmett's handmade, nine-string Freedom Guitar, no comment was made on his two-handed tapping, even though that was the only technique he employed. Alongside this final Cornucopia review is the headline "Beatles 2nd to Zeppelin," with an article listing Bob Dylan as the top male singer of 1970 and Joni Mitchell as the top female.

Leonard Feather wasn't the only music aficionado in the crowd at Shelly's for those last Cornucopia gigs. A young guitar player who was pushing musical boundaries in his own right was there, and he was far more impressed than the resident jazz critic. Lee Underwood was a studio player and a key member of folk singer Tim Buckley's groups. Although Buckley had long before established himself as a folk music icon, he too was a traveler, always looking for new sounds and new connections to music. By the early seventies, Buckley was entering his "Starsailor" period, which Underwood says had no reference points in the traditional LA jazz scene and avoided the continual recycling of blues clichés typically found in Hollywood's mainstream groups.

Underwood went to Shelly's to hear Kessel play and see if he had conceptually evolved. "To my delight," he says, "Barney had brought Emmett into his fold. Emmett was playing a nine-string Stick[14] then later a 10-string. The expansive sound and the potential of the instrument blew me away.

"It is to Kessel's credit that he saw the value of Emmett's Stick and showcased Emmett at that gig as part of his own service to young players and new musical styles. They played only standards that night, but I immediately introduced myself to Emmett and suggested he meet with Tim, as Tim was moving further into avant-garde concepts and contemporary classical modes. It seemed to me that The Stick offered enormous possibilities for Tim's new work. I told Tim about Emmett, brought them together, and Tim used Emmett on some of the gigs." Shortly after Underwood introduced Emmett to Tim, Chapman officially joined Buckley's band.

---

[14] Emmett was tapping on the Freedom Guitar at the time Underwood saw him with Kessel. He crafted the first true Stick prototype while playing with Buckley a few months later.

While Emmett's music may have run its course with Kessel's jazz, it found a new, welcoming and encouraging home with Buckley and the other Starsailors. "Tim was a fiery, ballsy, sensual, and often self-destructive guy," says Underwood, "while Emmett was more cerebral, cautious, and rationally constrained." The two were good foils for each other.

"I think Tim probably welcomed Emmett's outlook and approach," he continues, "regarding it as a complementary balance to his own, sometimes severe, excesses. Tim immediately saw The Stick's potential. He appreciated the fact that the Stick was new, that there was no precedent for it and that nobody knew how to play it. Emmett was still devising technical approaches, so nobody knew the scope of The Stick's possibilities. I remember Tim saying, 'It's too bad Emmett is the first, because he has to invent everything himself. That's not easy.' And Tim, of course, knew what he was talking about. He was inventing the whole Starsailor concept as he went along. There was nobody to help him or guide him or be his companion. Emmett occupied a similar position with the Stick."

Buckley's vision during the Starsailor period was to create music that alternated between drifting freely and forcing itself wherever it needed to go: music free of time, space and preconceived expectations, music in its purest, most elemental form. Emmett was on the same trip, discovering new music on his new instrument. The two were on similar musical planes, but more importantly, Tim was able to give Emmett the space sonically, physically and metaphysically, to explore what he was capable of with both hands tapping on the Freedom Guitar.

"Tim was exploring avant-garde approaches to music on several levels: odd-time signatures, new formal structures, the use of dissonance and new sounds in ways that preceded synthesizers and, most importantly, an entirely new vocal approach that had less to do with using the voice as a vehicle for conventional 'I-love-you-baby' lyrics and more to do with transforming the voice into an instrument capable of a vast range of non-verbal, tonal approaches to emotional expression," says Underwood. "Tim liked the fact that Emmett could play bass lines, chords and melodic lines simultaneously. So Tim let Emmett play bass lines and explore melodic and harmonic dissonance behind him. Tim's music was experimental and developmentally progressive, so Emmett's explorations were appropriate for that group, which included trombonist Glen Ferris and Janis Joplin's drummer, Maury Baker."

Buckley provided a playground for Emmett to truly let loose and with almost total freedom, explore his new technique and his evolving instrument. "Musically, I started from the outside and worked my way in," Emmett says. "It took me about two years into the playing technique to really concentrate on arranging songs. Before that, I was just raining down notes. There was always harmonic sense. I was always concerned with modes, scales and chords. It wasn't atonal, but sometimes it would get real close to atonal. I tried to have control of the modality and the harmonic factor. That still is the most important thing to me about music."

The Chapman and Buckley group jammed and performed in Los Angeles as a quintet, then traveled along the West Coast as a quartet. "We toured from Seattle down to San Diego," says Emmett. "We played about 15 concerts in various combinations. Buckley had been kind of a maverick. He was rebelling against his record label and that's why we played this really abstract, improvised music, just wild." Emmett provided bass-to-midrange-to-treble textures, a kind of sonic contextual cloud around Tim, who laid down harmonic/rhythmic foundations with his 12-string guitar and created a strong melodic focus with his octave-jumping vocal explorations. The music was exciting and adventurous for the players, but not always so for the audience.

Daily Variety, *Dec. 18, 1970:*

Nitery Reviews – Bitter End West

Tim Buckley and quintet, in for one frame, continue to delve into atonal, otherworldly sounds, with Buckley indulging himself in funky guitar playing and semi-vocalizing...

Severely disciplined group performed opening number, unidentified, for over 14 minutes, shredding the air. Bunk Gardener on tenor sax, bass clarinet, flute, flugelhorn; John Balkin on six-string bass; Maury Baker on tympani-drums and Emmett Chapman on nine-stringed guitar and semi-vocal-stringer. Sharps, flats, abrupt transitions, occasional on-mike shrieks and purrings by Buckley make up the second, 12-minute arrangement titled, according to Buckley, "You'll Know This Town By Its Graffiti." Might better be called "Monotony."

"Tim's Starsailor groups, particularly the one featuring John Balkin and the Gardner brothers, and a different group, featuring Emmett and trombonist Glenn Ferris, were simply too far-out for listeners who had loved Buckley's earlier, more conventional conceptual approaches to pop songs in general, and love songs in particular," says Underwood. "The new dissonance, the new non-verbal vocal extravaganzas, the new odd-time signatures, the rough, often chaotic clouds of madman improvisations, proved to be just too dense, complex, and demanding for nostalgia-oriented audiences that came to hear re-runs of [Buckley's hits] "Buzzin' Fly" or "Pleasant Street."

"The Balkin/Emmett groups presented their avant-garde performances in utmost purity. Sometimes the improvisations had momentum, focus, urgency, coherence and brilliance. Too often, they wandered around, lost cohesion, didn't go anywhere. As a result, record sales dropped off, fans turned away. Only small groups of dedicated listeners showed up. There was simply not enough economic support to pursue the concept any further. Tim gave more than three years to it. By 1972 or '73, it was time for a change, not only for economic reasons, but also because he needed to develop a new musical concept and renew his creative energies."

Audiences' reactions to Buckley's musical explorations were often contentious. "We would see it happen," Emmett recalls. "Tim would polarize and divide his audience. There would be those people who would be really grooving on what we were doing and other people who would walk out in disappointment that he wasn't playing his hit songs. He went much further than 'simply the artist not playing his hit songs.' He totally created a revolution in his own music. He was listening to Cecil Taylor, Thelonious Monk and Coltrane. He'd talk about them a lot. He wanted to intellectualize his music, which was almost uncharacteristic of him, but he wanted to occupy that space too. We played to a lot of hippies from the sixties, who were still devoted to him, and we got the most unusual reactions, really divided. Pretty amazing really."

In an April 1975 interview for *Goldmine Magazine*, Buckley commented on the Starsailor bands: "It was a lot of fun. I've got some tapes; it was fun to listen to, too. It was pretty adventurous because a singer hadn't done it[15]... In a lot of ways, it really was folk music; I'll always define that as folk music if a voice is involved. You're still trying to relate something but to relate out of a more holocaustal environment."

When asked later in the interview, "Speaking of people, are you still doing any work with Emmett Chapman, the inventor of The Stick?" Buckley responded, "That's in limbo for the time being, until I get a classical contract. Chapman is an amazing force. He's a musician that invented an instrument that works and that's pretty rare. We worked together for about eight months and it was terrific to a point. He fits into a segment of the classical things I've written, along with a choir of my own voice. These things are just different innovations that aren't displeasing to the ear; they're just odd. Anything that doesn't have a four-four bass line and a backbeat, fatback, is odd. That's why it's classical; it doesn't have a beat (laughs)."

Commercially, both Kessel's and Buckley's groups with Emmett fell short, but both gave Emmett the chance to get out and explore his instrument and his two-handed tapping technique with other musicians who supported, encouraged and drove him forward. They provided a living laboratory for musical exploration, where boundary pushing was the norm. If he needed proof that he was on the right path, Kessel and Buckley provided that proof. "Emmett's Stick offered infinite possibilities," Underwood says. "I knew Emmett's fresh, original instrument and his unique technical approaches would enhance Tim's context, which is why I brought Emmett to Tim in the first place."

"It didn't seem very commercially successful," says Emmett, "but playing with Tim Buckley seemed like a *real* opportunity. More than

---

[15] 'It' refers to Buckley atonally exploring his 5 ½ octave vocal range.

that, he seemed like a phenomenon to me. The best singer I'd ever heard, the best musician – a rare gift to the planet. I really regarded him highly, as far as his talent goes. I felt honoured to be playing with him. Everybody who knew Tim thought he was larger than life, and it wasn't just because he was famous. It was just from watching him in action, getting people to do what he wanted without even saying anything. It was a behaviour-oriented approach, rather than lecturing, preaching, analyzing. I'm very analytical and he would just put me down when I did that. He didn't want to hear it. It's sort of like the James Dean approach to being heroic, but not really talking about it. He wanted to be heroic. He was just a little guy, but he'd carry my amplifiers. He would do the hard work, daredevil things too, things he thought were dangerous, James Dean style. He didn't want to hear about responsibility. He was a real rebel."

As Emmett's music was evolving with Kessel and Buckley, so too was his instrument. As the two-parallel-hand tapping technique became more and more comfortable, limitations with the Freedom Guitar soon emerged. Armed with a new technique and a new performance medium, Emmett hit the wood shop. The irony was clear: he already knew how he needed to play. The technique was in place from the very beginning. All he needed was the right instrument with which to play.

He started by crafting a long, thin, Macassar Ebony board, rectangular in every dimension, which looked like a long guitar neck with no body. Macassar Ebony is a "sensual black and brown striped Southeast Asian wood, naturally heavy and oily, needing no finish," says Emmett. Since there was no picking or strumming, only tapping, there was no need for a body. The superfluous was cut away. Only what added to the fluidity, expressiveness and power of his technique remained. A standard electric guitar pickup was mounted inside a small ebony box and suspended above the strings, near the bottom tailpiece. A mount near the bottom of the board held the instrument in place by hooking onto a belt worn around the waist. A strap worn under the arm, coming across the chest and around the back, held the board in place from the top. This was the first official 'Stick.' Emmett christened the instrument "The Electric Stick."

(Emmett and The Electric Stick. Photo by Dan Chapman)

The Electric Stick made its sonic debut with the Buckley groups but had its real coming out party with the press in the February 1972 issue of *Overture*, the American Federation of Musicians, Local 47 monthly publication, under the headline: "The Only 'Electric Stick' In the Directory." This was the first time that Emmett's Stick drew headline attention. Like so many future articles about Sticks and Stick players, the *Overture* article begins with a question: "What has nine strings, three amplifiers, and sounds like a harpsichord, piano, steel guitar and electric bass?" And then, once again with uncanny foreshadowing, *Overture* reads: "The electric stick, of course, an invention of member Emmett Chapman." The accompanying picture shows Emmett with the Electric Stick: nine strings, ebony board with the pickup mounted in a box and suspended above the strings. The Freedom Guitar had evolved into The Stick. In the photo, Emmett is playing. His mouth is slightly open, his head slightly tilted back. His hands are evenly spaced. The technique and the instrument are both in place. This article is important. It marks the first public acknowledgement that Emmett isn't a guitar player. It confirms that he is playing something different than a guitar, and it focuses on his two-handed tapping. The instrument is no longer a modified guitar like The Freedom Guitar. The Electric Stick is an entity unto itself. Emmett has also come to the fore as a solo artist and featured member of the Buckley group; a significant departure point, where Emmett and his Stick are strong enough, exciting enough and perhaps valid enough to stand on their own.

"The stick is hooked into the belt and played with both hands on the strings—piano style," the article reads, focusing on the playing technique. "Chapman feels that the sound ranges across all music disciplines and is applicable in rock, jazz or classical music. 'I'm trying for the piano-harpsichord but with a little bit of Jimmie (sic) Hendrix,' opines the inventor-musician." The article continues. "The sound was bold and fascinating... Chapman makes a lot of music with the stick; it has a haunting quality yet elements of electric bass. You have to hear it to understand this."

EMMETT CHAPMAN plays the Electric Stick, his own invention, in a demonstration at Local 47. It's the only such instrument mentioned in the Local 47 directory.

(Emmett in *Overture*, February 1972.)

Although the article makes mention of Emmett as a member of Buckley's group, this marks the beginning of Emmett's journey as a solo musician. By April, Emmett would indeed be travelling solo with his Stick, playing with support from only a drummer, Bob Conti, at

Jazz West in Los Angeles. The *Nitery Review* for those shows states, "it's an ingenious invention with a fascinating sound and considerable potential." The pieces are falling into place. In the photo that accompanies this article Emmett looks ready to head out on his own with his Stick firmly in hand and take on the world. According to the article, The Electric Stick sounds like it's ready too.

The nine-stringed, suspended-pickup Electric Stick worked in essence. The sound was rich and unique and Emmett's tapping was fully realized on this slimmed down, re-envisioned Freedom Guitar. But the creation, design and search for the perfect instrument to fully exploit two-handed tapping continued. A new prototype was made. It was longer and wider than the original Electric Stick and constructed out of Ironwood, rather than Macassar Ebony. The suspended pickup was replaced with a regular electric guitar-type pickup, mounted underneath the strings. Emmett replaced the violin-type tuning pegs he had previously used, with standard guitar tuners. Another string was added to the bass side. Now each side of The Stick had five strings – balance. Like the Freedom Guitar and Electric Stick, the lowest strings still ran up the middle of the new design, splitting the instrument into two equal halves. This new version had 26 frets and four circular mother-of-pearl inlays, evenly spaced five frets apart that marked off a set of interval relationships between the frets and the strings.

"Making it longer, wider and adding an extra string turned it into a whole new instrument," says Emmett. This whole new instrument, still called The Electric Stick, looked much more like the present day Chapman Stick. Once again, Lee Underwood played a major role in getting the news out about Emmett and The Stick.

"My trip with Tim, from the beginning, during all our years together," says Underwood, "was a giving of myself in service to him and the music. Emmett was one of my 'gifts' to Tim. Later on, in 1973, it seemed to me that Emmett's innovative brilliance should be celebrated on its own terms. In service to him and his music and The Stick, I interviewed him for *The LA Weekly*, letting people know he was doing good things. I hope it helped." Lee's full-page feature on Emmett and The Stick for the *Los Angeles Weekly News* ran on October 15, 1973. He writes:

Guitar players watch out! Emmett Chapman is on the scene with his ten-string Electric Stick!

It's got ten strings, but it's not a guitar.

It covers nearly the entire piano range (down to low C, up to C above high C), but it's not a piano.

Emmett Chapman invented it and constructed it, and he's played it with such notable performers as Barney Kessel and Tim Buckley. He plays everything on it—bass lines, chords, and melodies.

And after all that, he is even modest: "It's not meant to replace the guitar or the piano—but it is an alternative."

A modest assessment for the massive and varied tones he produces with this extraordinary invention that sounds more like a celestial choir with balls.

Underwood described the instrument's sound:

I was astonished by the variety of tones and moods he produced with it. At first, clear and full, like a deep, rich guitar. Then a gutsy fuzz tone with ferocious, Hendrix-like wah-wah punctuations, followed by a softer, muted effect, similar to an organ or electric piano. He also created blues sounds, with bass lines like Jack Bruce and dirty melodic lines comparable to B. B. King's. The range and combinations of sounds Chapman creates seems endless.

The article offered insight into the mindset that created the technique, the instrument and the music. In Underwood's story Emmett states:

> *"I've never been able to copy lines and turn them into licks like a lot of people do. But I can get involved with the conceptual approach, the mood of a piece. You know, get it on a feeling level, then put my own system to work."*

Emmett's own system was quickly leading him away from a sideman's role and into the world of a solo player and bandleader.

> *"Now I can do it all," he continues in the article. "I'm learning how to create and plan my own bass lines on a new instrument, using odd time signatures—9/4, 13/4, 5/4, 7/8, etc. It's these new signatures that have led me directly to composition.*
>
> *"I hated writing tunes. You know, standard things for standard-oriented groups. But now I generate rhythms with my left hand, and those rhythms in turn generate the creative energy—I respond to them and compose off of them.*
>
> *"And if I control the bass lines, then I control all the directions—I can abruptly change time or key or mood and not have to worry about dragging out for an hour playing just one chord. I can state the bass rhythms, state the chords like a rhythm guitar, and independently state all the melodies as well. With just a drummer, I can do what a whole group can do."*

The accompanying photo shows Emmett with the new Stick prototype in performance at The Cellar with Les DeMerle. There is a recording of that show. Emmett sounds like an entire jazz-rock fusion band, all by himself. He and DeMerle are playing blistering lines and pushing each other on. The interplay between the two leaps off the tapes. In the photo, Emmett is looking off to the left, an inquisitive, searching look on his face. It's as if he's searching for the next chord or the next direction to jump off. The Stick looks almost like the modern Sticks. Emmett is starting to look like the Emmett of today as well. In the February '72 *Overture* article, Emmett has his trademark beard, high forehead and "granny-glasses," as Underwood calls them, but his hair is long, beard shaggy and the traces of grey that have gradually taken over his hair don't show. In the photo from Underwood's article, a little over a year later, Emmett has matured. He looks confident with his instrument. Emmett's hair and beard are still on the long side, but trimmed and neat. The now familiar scattering of grey creates an almost sage-like look. He looks strong and healthy. The Stick looks more at home with its belt hook tucked into the top of his pants and the shoulder strap securely holding the top of the instrument in place. The Stick looks ready for its big introduction to the world and so does Emmett.

Underwood wraps up his article with:

He's an inventor, a carpenter, and electrician. He's also a student, using his G. I. Bill to study more electronics. And above all, he's one of the most exciting yet-to-be-heard musicians and composers on the scene today... Once you've heard Chapman and his Electric Stick, you'll never be the same. Happy Listening!

(Emmett at Les DeMerle's, 1973. Photo by Dan Chapman)

Chapter 8 – Pick Up Your Stick and Walk the Earth

Two reviews from Emmett's first trips to New York with The Stick:

"HELD OVER AT TWO SAINTS, EMMETT 'THE STICK' CHAPMAN & FRIENDS: There is John McLaughlin, there was Jimi Hendrix, but now there is Emmett 'The Stick' Chapman, who is following McLaughlin and Hendrix in a direct linear evolution. However, Chapman's instrument, The Chapman Stick, is not merely a new kind of guitar but an instrument that combines the best of bass and guitar with five touch-tone strings of each that are played without picking or plucking, in fact what Chapman is now doing with this new instrument is just as important as the improvisations and compositions John Coltrane was creating in the 1960s."

> *-J.C. Thomas, author* Chasin' The Trane

"It looks like what's left after you hit somebody over the head with a guitar," she whispered to her father. "But I really like the way it sounds."

> *-Morag Musk (14 year-old audience member at the Museum of Modern Art, NYC, 1974)*

Emmett had played the California scene. His résumé was impressive. Barney Kessel and Tim Buckley had given him immediate validation in musical circles and fertile laboratories in which to explore his instrument and his music. His two-handed tapping technique was evolving, becoming stronger and more intricate every day. He had the support of his family. The next logical step was to hit the road. Where was the obvious place to go? Where would The Stick take its next steps from a personal endeavour to one that excited and inspired other players? "Simple," says Emmett. "New York."

Before heading to New York, Emmett had already decided to build Sticks and sell them to other musicians. The attention in the press, the responses from the Buckley and Kessel gigs and the reactions to his solo shows were more than enough to get adventurous musicians excited, not only about Emmett's music, but also about the music they could make with Sticks of their own. Others wanted a piece of the action.

On a trip to San Francisco in early 1973, Emmett met an instrument builder who had a stockpile of ironwood. Ironwood is a very dense and stable wood, much like the ebony he had used previously for the Electric Stick. It was perfect. Inspired by what he calls "the legitimate, self-sufficient, communal attitude that could still be found in San Francisco at the time," he started construction on six instruments destined for sale, two from the San Francisco ironwood.

The garage in Chapman's Yucca Trail home became the official workshop. Emmett did the woodwork, fretwork, electronics and setup on each instrument. The rest of the Chapmans pitched in too. Yuta continued working at Occidental Insurance to support the family, but she also became the official business manager for Emmett and the emerging Stick business. She booked shows, arranged travel plans for Emmett and handled the office and financial affairs of the company, as The Stick quickly moved from a passion to a business. Even daughters Diana and Grace were called into service. Diana remembers gluing electric guitar pickups into the ironwood pickup housings of the early Sticks in the Chapman bathroom. The bathroom was the cleanest place in the house and dust free – dust being the nemesis of electric guitar pickups.

With Sticks on his workbench, Emmett left for New York. The unfinished instruments would have to wait for his return. He made three trips to New York City over the following year. His music was enthusiastically embraced. One of his first stops was at the legendary 5-Spot in Greenwich Village. The mandate at the 5-Spot was innovation. Thelonious Monk, Roland Kirk, Eric Dolphy and Charles Mingus had all called the club home. Early performances of groups led by Coltrane and Ornette Coleman had graced the club's stage. Emmett stepped into the spotlight and wowed the crowd.

As in LA, musicians were the first to take notice. At one show, Joe Zawinul had wandered in to check out this new musician in town. Zawinul had already made a name for himself working with Miles Davis on Davis's landmark albums *Bitches Brew* and *In a Silent Way*. He had formed his own progressive jazz group, Weather Report, in 1971 and was well on his way to establishing his place in the progressive jazz pantheon.

Zawinul arrived late at the packed club. Emmett was well into his second set, but he immediately liked what he heard. After the show he introduced himself to Emmett and asked to try The Stick. Zawinul picked it up, climbed up on a table and with much gusto and showmanship, tapped away. He wailed away with reckless abandon, and no clue technically of what he was doing, but it sounded great. The rest of Emmett's band joined in and off they went on an impromptu concert. Emmett was stunned. It was his turn to be blown away by The Stick and how a gifted musician like Zawinul could pull off incredible sounds relying soley on sheer intuition and creativity. Immediately, Zawinul placed an order for a Stick of his own.

Emmett played all around New York and in clubs in Greenwich Village and as had been the case years earlier in Germany, word quickly spread. This time, it wasn't 'The American Guitarist with the Weird Guitar,' but 'The Guy from LA Playing That Weird Stick-Thing.' The 5-Spot changed its name to The Two Saints and reviewer Peter Occhiogrosso wrote:

Soho Weekly News, *July 1974*

Emmett "The Stick" Chapman and Friends – Peter Occhiogrosso

If the electric guitar and later the electric piano changed not only jazz history but the entire music scene over the next 35 years, then what of an instrument that combines the salient aspects of both electric guitar and piano in one body that is eminently suited for playing through a whole range of electronic equipment from the standard phase-shifters and wah-wahs to the most advanced ARP synthesizer?

Occhiogrosso goes on to describe The Stick and the two-handed tapping method and then continues:

Although The Stick has been given a good workout here lately at local spots like the 2 SAINTS on St. Mark's Place and radio stations WKCR and WRVR, it really has not yet received the kind of national attention such a marvellously simple but immense development deserves. That should change now that Emmett is on his way back to LA to put the finishing touches on his patented design and build a few more for anxious customers. Among those who have already placed their orders are Joe Zawinul of Weather Report, Gil Evans, Steve Howe of Yes and Gabor Szabo. Also interested are Robby Krieger, the Beach Boys and John McLaughlin. What's interesting about that list isn't merely the cross-section of musicians from all different levels of electric

116

music, rock and jazz, but the fact that two of them are keyboard players.

It was Emmett and his music alone that inspired such a diverse cross section of musician – he was the only Stick player in world! The New York critic had more to say about Emmett and The Stick:

But The Stick does not seem to be just another technological addendum, like Herbie Hancock piling layer on layer of electronic keyboards over his basic piano and then doing nothing with it all. Zawinul himself seems to feel that it could restore some of the personal warmth that gets lost in the equally prodigious electronic set-up he uses with Weather Report (to much greater effect than Herbie, it goes without saying). And Chapman is the first to admit that in the hands of more experienced musicians than himself, the total potential of the Stick would be beyond what he is able to produce on it now...

Those who have heard Emmett and not been knocked out should reserve judgment until the next Charlie Christian picks one up and plays it. The real question isn't what Chapman can do on it but what Hendrix could have done, what Zawinul and Gil Evans will do with the potentially most important development of the decade in the realm of electric music.

Occhiogrosso made some interesting observations. First, that The Stick was in a different family and had far more potential than sound-layering electronic instruments like the synthesizer. Secondly, that the phenomenal potential for the instrument lay not only in Emmett's hands, but also in the hands of players who were yet to pick up Sticks and find their own music.

Emmett would soon return to Los Angeles and finish building the first Sticks. A patent had been applied for and granted, and orders were starting to come in. Emmett missed his family and longed for home. But first, there were still important and pivotal New York gigs to play before he returned to the West Coast.

On September 20th and 21st, 1974, Emmett played at Summergarden in the Abby Aldrich Rockefeller Sculpture Garden at the Museum of Modern Art. The Summergarden series began a few years earlier with the mandate to "enhance the artistic life of New York city." Virtuosi from Julliard, Jazz at Lincoln Centre and composers and musicians from around the world have performed there, and continue to perform in the sculpture garden today. The press release for Emmett's shows reads: "Chapman's music has been called 'compositional-improvisation.' It is stylistically eclectic and employs The Stick's technical and dynamic range from Bachian counterpoint, Eastern sitar-like bass drones, blues note-bending and 'walking' bass, to intricate free-form jazz improvisation and explosive rock effects."

Michael Hechtman covered the MoMA gigs for *The New York Post*. Under the headline "The Greatest Thing Since the Piano" Hechtman tells the story of 14 year-old Morag Musk:

> *In a decade or so, after the world of music is revolutionized, Morag Musk will be able to tell her children she was there when history was made.*
>
> *She'll relate to them how she was 14 and visiting New York from Cheshire England when she wondered into a museum and became one of the first people in the world to hear the "Chapman Stick," which its inventor says, represents "a major juncture in the evolution of musical instruments."*
>
> *She may also recall her reaction when she first saw and heard the "Stick."*

"It looks like what's left after you hit somebody over the head with a guitar," she whispered to her father. *"But I really like the way it sounds."*

Hechtman recorded other people's reactions to Emmett's music. Museum employee, Gilbert Robinson, was working on the fourth floor when he heard Emmett's music drifting up from the sculpture garden below. He was drawn to the garden for a closer look. "It's beautiful," he said. "I've never heard anything like it." Mrs. Sandra Trevan, a "proper-looking middle-aged lady quietly contemplating the sculpture," said that Emmett's music "does not assault the ears." Luis Garcia-Ponce, visiting the museum from Mexico City added, "It's what I would expect to find in a museum like this, in a city like this. It's strange and beautiful and amazing."

"I played "Eleanor Rigby" at the Museum," says Emmett. "There was a lot of improvisation. All of my tunes gave a lot of windows for improvisation. I tried to have a harmonic theme that would be compatible, but had a lot of improv. I played "Yesterday" by the Beatles, I probably played "Jesu, Joy of Man's Desiring." I played an original composition that I called "Bells, Echoes and Avalanches." Coltrane inspired that tune and it was very much like what I did later with "My Favorite Things." I did another original tune called "Weather Permitting." A Wayne Shorter horn solo from *Weather Report* inspired me, so to credit that I called it "Weather Permitting." And of course I did lots of improvised music in and around those structured original tunes. The improvisation was always the best part of what I did."

Success and opportunity continued to follow Emmett in New York. Musical connections were made, people heard him play. Emmett was even offered several recording contracts. Vanguard Records and the legendary John Hammond, among others, offered Emmett recording deals but he turned them down. "They were great offers," Emmett says. "But for some reason, I wasn't ready to capitalize on them yet." Upon reflection he adds, "I failed to appreciate the significance of them at the time."

When Emmett arrived in New York, his instrument was the Electric Stick. The name reflected the simplicity and forthrightness of the design. No extra levers or extraneous parts – only the functional necessities. It took some convincing, particularly from his mother, but eventually he added his own name to his instrument. The Electric Stick was now The Chapman Stick, and on September 3rd, 1974 it all became official:

United States Patent #3,833,751. Sept. 3, 1974

Chapman

GUITAR-LIKE INSTRUMENT WITH MAGNETIC PICKUP

Inventor: **Emmett H. Chapman,** *8320 Yucca Trl., Los Angeles, Calif. 90046*

Filed : **Feb. 22, 1973**

Appl. No.: **334859**

Primary Examiner—Richard B. Wilkinson

Assistant Examiner—Stanley J. Witkowski

Attorney, Agent or Firm—Miketta, Glenny, Poms & Smith

ABSTRACT

An electric guitar having a body of generally rectangular cross-section and consisting essentially of an elongated fretted wooden fingerboard, a headpiece extending upwardly therefrom, and a tailpiece extending downwardly therefrom. A set of tuned strings, preferably nine in number, extends in parallel relation immediately above and out of contact with the frets, in line substantially parallel to the fretted face of the fingerboard, the strings being anchored to the tailpiece and each string being attached to an individual tensioning member forming part of the headpiece. A magnetic pickup assembly is carried by the tailpiece, including an individual magnetic pickup in operative relation with each of the strings. The instrument is light in weight, and is supported by a bracket or hook engageable with the user's belt and by a strap around the user's neck and upper chest, the strap being attached to the instrument at or adjacent to the headpiece, whereby to maintain the instrument in correct playing position, upwardly more nearly vertically and across the user's torso, and freeing the user's hands from the need of supporting the instrument. The user is thereby enabled to execute unusual musical effects with the fingers of both hands engaging selected strings, against selected frets of the fingerboard during play. In the preferred form of the invention having nine strings, the strings are uniquely tuned as follows: A first, highest pitched string; a second string tuned a perfect fourth interval below the first string; a third string tuned a perfect fourth interval below the second string; a fourth string tuned a perfect fourth interval below the third string; a fifth string tuned a perfect fourth interval below the fourth string; a sixth, lowest bass string tuned a major seventh interval below the fifth string; a seventh string tuned a perfect fifth interval above the sixth string; an eighth string tuned a perfect fifth interval above the seventh string; and a ninth string tuned a perfect fifth interval above the eighth string. The first five strings constitute a melody group, and the remaining four strings constitute a bass and chord group.

BACKGROUND AND FIELD OF THE INVENTION

The present invention relates generally to musical instruments, and more particularly to an electric guitar of simplified construction having nine tensioned strings tuned in a unique manner.

Instruments of the guitar family are characterized by the provision of an elongated fretted fingerboard having a plurality of tensioned strings immediately above the fingerboard, and means for amplifying the musical note produced by the vibrations of the strings when actuated as by being plucked by a plectrum or the user's fingers. In electric guitars, the sound amplifying means include a set of magnetic pickups, each pickup being close to a string and the electrical outputs of the pickups are fed to electric amplifier devices of many different kinds. The electric guitar of the present invention is of the latter type, and has a body, preferably wooden of generally rectangular cross-section consisting essentially of an elongated fretted fingerboard, a headpiece...

When played, the fingers of both of the users' hands tapping the strings and holding them against selected frets, increases the chordal melodic, and contrapuntal possibilities for producing a full, orchestral sound. By having his two hands free to engage nine strings, the performer is enabled to play bass, chords, and melody simultaneously. There are strings for left-hand chords on both sides of the lowest pitched bass string (the sixth string in the series of nine). Normally, on this instrument chords are executed with the five strings tuned in intervals of fourths on one side of the lowest bass string, together with the three strings tuned in intervals of fifths on the other side of that bass string. Melody, however, is played almost exclusively on the first five strings tuned in fourth intervals. In effect, there are two groupings of strings partially overlapping the register covered. Melody played with the right hand in the upper portion of the fingerboard necessarily cancels out some of the notes on the left-hand chord in this method of two-handed tapping. Thus the three strings not used for melody help to create the effect of the chord sustaining over the melody line...

...Accordingly, it is a principal object of the present invention to provide a novel construction of an electric guitar, and the provision thereon of nine novelly tuned strings. Additional objects and purposes are to provide, in such an instrument, an elongated body, preferably of wood, of generally cross-section and including...

Emmett left New York musically charged and with orders for Chapman Sticks. As Peter Occhiogrosso wrote, Joe Zawinul, Gil Evans, Steve Howe, Todd Rundgren, Gabor Szabo, Robby Krieger, the Beach Boys and John McLaughlin were all interested in Sticks. Those six Sticks that Emmett had started before he went to New York were waiting in the garage of his Yucca Trail home. He headed back to California to finish them up.

Chapter 9 – Stick Enterprises Takes Flight

"The Stick* fulfills a musician's aspiration to play bass lines, keyboard harmonies, and lead instrumental lines, all at the same time.

"The long, free melody lines of jazz guitar, and the blazing expression of rock lead, can be structured from the bass on up through the chords, giving harmonic meaning and rhythmic depth to the melody.

"The bass is strong and supportive, with the bottom drive of electric bass and the high frequency attack and overtones of acoustic bass. The chordal possibilities are as free, polytonal, and infinite as those available to the keyboard artist."

*THE STICK and THE CHAPMAN STICK TOUCHBOARD are registered trademarks of Stick Enterprises, Inc.

-From an early Stick promotional brochure.

Back in LA, Emmett needed to finish those first commercially available Sticks. He also had a business to create that would manufacture instruments, educate people and promote both The Stick and his two-handed tapping technique. The Chapman garage became the woodworking shop and the bathroom the electronics workshop. Yuta ran the business end, Grace and Diana pitched in and Emmett balanced it all: teaching his technique, building new instruments, working on his music, promoting both himself and The Stick and juggling his family life.

By the end of 1974, in addition to the early gigs with Kessel and Buckley, Emmett had countless performances both as a solo artist and as the lead in small combos. He had finished two film scores and recorded with guitarist James Lee Stanley on his album *Three's the Charm*. He was appearing regularly with the jazz-rock group Transfusion at The Cellar and continued playing solo and in duos with drummers all around LA.

The music press continued to take notice. The November 1974 issues of two major music industry magazines featured in-depth articles on Emmett and The Stick. November's *Guitar Player* magazine featured a young Carlos Santana[16] on the cover. Legendary studio bassist and teacher, Carol Kaye, had a column on page 50 titled "Improvisations." Kessel himself had an "Ask Barney Kessel" feature on page 52. On page 16, a photo of Emmett dressed in a white shirt and white pants with Stick prototype number three, sits in the lower left-hand corner. Above the photo, in the upper left corner, in a soft, sixties psychedelic font is the headline, "The Electric Stick!" and the sub-heading, "A guitar & then some."

Guitar Player was the leading guitar publication at the time. Such a major feature in such a major magazine was like a grand slam home run for Emmett and the newly born Stick. Daniel Sawyer's article gives an overview of The Stick, highlights Emmett's discovery of the technique, and goes on to list his accomplishments to date. He notes:

> *The audience response to The Stick has been fantastic. After a concert, curious musicians are always sure to be seen asking Emmett all sorts of questions concerning this new instrument. A blind saxophonist, who heard Emmett play solo at the* Troubadour *in Los Angeles, came up afterwards to ask how many musicians were in his "group!"*

The article goes on to mention Emmett's plans to manufacture and sell the instruments "on a large scale eventually." The first Sticks

---

[16] Alphonso Johnson would later play Stick with Santana.

cost $550 plus $75 for the case, with a $200 deposit in advance for materials. Sawyer concluded:

> *Such a totally unique instrument in the hands of such a talented and original musician is one of those rare artistic combinations that comes along seldom in a decade. But such is Emmett Chapman and his Electric Stick.*

In much the same way that playing with musicians like Tim Buckley and Barney Kessel gave Emmett's music instant legitimacy, Daniel Sawyer's *Guitar Player* article provided industry credibility for The Stick. Guitar players, from aspiring to professional, read (and continue to read) *Guitar Player*. The Stick was quickly becoming the real deal.

The iconic jazz magazine *Downbeat* came next. While *Guitar Player* spoke to musicians in general, and guitar players specifically, *Downbeat* spoke to players and fans alike about the cream of the jazz scene. The November 21, 1974 edition ran a short feature on Emmett and his music, highlighting his gigs at Two Saints in New York. The un-credited article compared Emmett to Thelonious Monk, Roland Kirk, Eric Dolphy and once again John Coltrane, providing more legitimacy and validation for Emmett and The Stick.

On the same New York trip when *Downbeat* reviewed the Two Saints gigs, The Stick made its debut on national television. A well-dressed Chapman, complete with billowy white shirt, strode onto the stage in front of television cameras and a nation-wide audience, and wrote his name "Emmett Chapman" on a board, while the theme music to *What's My Line* played in the background. The *What's My Line* panellists, Soupy Sales, Gene Shalit, Beverly Sills and Arlene Francis were stumped. "Is it wood?" "Is it electrical?" "Does it produce something?" they asked. "They got everything, but they couldn't figure out that the Chapman Stick was a musical instrument," said Emmett. For baffling the panel, Emmett won a drawing set, which he gave to Diana and Grace and was paid a small fee for performing the Beatles song "Yesterday." Playing before a primetime nationwide television audience was the real prize though.

By the early months of 1975, Emmett had appeared on national television, performed his museum concerts, gigged at landmark jazz clubs and performed on national radio. He had also secured a clinic and direct sales agreement with Sam Ash Music and had received recording offers from both Impulse and Vanguard Records.

Paul Ash, co-owner with his brother Jerry, of the Sam Ash stores heard that Emmett would be performing at MoMA. The brothers attended the show and were blown away. Afterwards, they introduced themselves to Emmett. "We were doing a big expo at the time," Ash says, "just that weekend, so we invited him to come and demonstrate. He came and we set him up near the entrance. Everybody was fascinated, and we decided to try selling the instrument. He would come and give demonstrations for us. We'd advertise it and we sold a number of Sticks, not huge numbers, but one piece at a time." Sam Ash was the first Stick retailer.

"It was phenomenal to hear one player playing the melody, the chords, the rhythm, everything all at one time," Ash continues. "He had a great facility for that instrument. I guess he was born to play it, especially since he gave birth to it."

Downbeat ran another, more in-depth Stick feature in September 1975, titled "How to understand The Stick," written by noted jazz educator Dr. William Fowler. The article featured the first published Stick lesson. Dr. Fowler wrote about The Stick, explained Emmett's two-handed technique, how to hold The Stick and described basic playing techniques. *Downbeat* added a "Music Workshop" column written by Emmett titled "A Sticky Blues." Emmett's Sticky Blues lesson featured the blues scale played with the right hand and a challenging chord progression in the left. Once again, support from *Downbeat* gave instant credibility and international exposure to Emmett, his music and The Stick.

In a sad twist, in the same issue of *Downbeat,* along with Dr. Fowler's Stick article, Lee Underwood contributed a brief item in the magazine's "Final Bar" section. The "Final Bar" means obituaries, in jazz. This obituary was for Timothy Charles Buckley III. Emmett's friend and musical co-explorer, Tim Buckley, died on June 29, 1975, in Santa Monica. He was only 28 years old. He accomplished more than he was ever given credit for, including providing a creative laboratory for Emmett to explore and refine The Stick and his two-handed parallel string tapping technique and the second major opportunity for Emmett to show the world The Chapman Stick.

Back in California, Emmett got busy. The New York exposure resulted in nearly 30 orders for the $550 Sticks (plus $75 for the hardshell case). After the woodworking in the garage and electronics building in the bathroom, Emmett would use the two bathroom sinks as a makeshift workbench, laying Sticks across them while he worked on the final set-ups and fine-tuning. Finally, the first Stick rolled off the makeshift production line. Emmett and his brother Dan took Stick number 101 up into the hills above LA. Emmett triumphantly raised it above his head, with the sprawling urban landscape of Los Angeles spread out below him, like a foreign land awaiting conquest. As Emmett held The Stick up, Dan snapped a photo: "Stick Above LA." That first instrument is still safely stored at Stick Enterprises.

(Stick Above LA. Photo by Dan Chapman.)

The second Stick ended up with Tony Eldridge, Emmett's neighbour on Yucca Trail. Joe Zawinul got the third. The fourth "went to a Moonie, who later gave it away to the Sun Myung Moon Organization," says Emmett. The final instruments went to Paul and Jerry Ash to be sold at Sam Ash Music.

(Tony Eldridge and Emmett, 1975.)

But musical instruments don't play themselves. As sleek, streamlined and efficient as The Stick looked, people would never have been inspired to pick up Sticks and tap if Emmett hadn't been playing them. The artist creates the instrument. Emmett was driven by his music to play, and he played his Stick wherever he could. The routine went something like this: Emmett would head out on the road (music stores and colleges were frequent stops) and come home with a list of orders. In the local Bloomington, Indiana newspaper, *Primo Times,* Bob Slone wrote of a typical Chapman Stick performance/seminar on November 10, 1975:

"Emmett Chapman came to Bloomington last weekend to demonstrate his remarkable invention, The Stick. His performance at the Monroe County Library with I. U. music student Peter Erskine[17] on drums, was memorable. Emmett's Stick, with the aid of his virtuoso technique, was most impressive... It's the most versatile instrument I've ever heard, producing the sounds of the bass, piano, organ, saxophone, electric guitar, acoustic guitar, and even the drums beautifully."

Emmett would usually present a three-part show, starting with a set of music, then a brief description of The Stick with a question and answer period, followed by another set of music. The music was always the event's driving force. Emmett was promoting himself as an artist first and foremost. He would grab the crowd with his playing, then reveal what was going on behind the wizard's curtain. Slone continues:

"Through all these songs, he played with not only great chops, but also with an energy and creativity that might establish Emmett as the '70's first great innovator.

---

[17] Later a world-renowned drummer and musician in his own right.

"As he performs, he nods his face up to the audience occasionally with the look of a chemistry professor standing over a rack of test tubes saying, 'Look what happens when you mix these two together.'"

During the lecture portion of the show, Emmett demonstrated how easy it was to actually tap the strings down and hold them against the frets. He broke down the left hand chord technique and the right hand melody. In Indiana, he chose an organ sound and turned a simple chord progression into a "swinging, hip blues." Next, he would talk about the tuning: how the bass tuning in ascending fifths, played from the middle of The Stick outward, led to all sorts of new chord sounds and bass line patterns. He also explained how you could transpose chord shapes, not only vertically like on a guitar, but also horizontally across the frets.

Once again, Sloan was impressed:

"The seminar helped to alleviate the feeling that The Stick had but one drawback: that it would take the genius of the man who invented it to be able to play it. The ingenious simplicity of his system makes The Stick accessible to a person of average intelligence, but not without many hours of practice. This is typical of most musical instruments."

Bob Culbertson was a 20 year-old guitar player in San Jose who saw one of Emmett's early concerts. Five months later, he had his first Stick. "I was teaching guitar at Guitar Showcase," he says. "A bunch of my friends and I walked into the store on a Saturday and we heard this noise coming from upstairs, like a rumble. The guys in the store said, 'You've got to go upstairs and check out this clinic.' I was on my way to the beach and I really wasn't interested, but a couple of people said, 'No, you've really got to see this. It's kind of like a guitar, but it is way cooler.' I thought it was a synthesizer and I wasn't much into that, so I said, 'No, I'll check it out later.' Finally, a buddy of mine who I played with in a band got insistent and said, 'No! Just go up there and look for a minute, then you guys can go and do whatever you need to do.'

"So I went up and I saw Emmett play. He had just started his clinic. I didn't leave. I told someone to go and get the rest of my friends to come up. Fortunately they were into it. So we just sat and watched the whole thing. As soon as it was over, I knew I wanted to buy one.

"At the time I was experimenting a bit with playing piano. And there was a guy out at the flea market in San Jose who played two guitars at the same time, but it was a very limited tapping method that he did. I was experimenting with tapping on my guitar a little bit, but nowhere near like the concept of what Emmett was doing. As soon as I saw Emmett, the whole thing came together."

After five distinctly different instrument prototypes, Stick Enterprises was incorporated, and in 1974 the first Chapman Sticks were offered for sale. The change in the Chapman family's life was irreversible. From 1969 to 1974 Emmett was the only Stick player in the world. By the end of 1976 he had 220 Stick playing companions, but Emmett still very much led the way. He was, by far, the most active public Stick performer. He also taught over 50 Stick students directly and about 150 more by correspondence. Emmett may have cut the first path through the two-handed parallel string tapping forest but others would quickly start clearing trails of their own.

While the big name musicians like Joe Zawinul and Gil Evans were there at the beginning and were among the first to tap Sticks of their own, it was a host of lesser-known musicians, support players and amateurs who would explore The Stick and push the instrument's musical boundaries. Almost organically, from a grassroots level, it was the backline musicians who brought The Stick into their bands and onto the bandstands in the instrument's early days.

Don Schiff was among the first. He played bass in the Las Vegas show band and club scene in the early seventies:

> **Jim Reilly:** *You got your first Stick in '75?*
>
> **Don Schiff:** *Yeah, I think so.*
>
> **JR:** *That was pretty much the beginning of The Stick.*
>
> **DS:** *Yeah, I guess so. It was a really, really low number, within the first hundred Sticks.*
>
> *Of course, I lived in Vegas and Emmett was in California, so I bought it and I took a lesson from Emmett to learn how to tap it instead of trying to pluck it or blow it like a clarinet. I thought I'd approach it like any other instrument and learn where the notes were and play it. I'd spent all this time learning where the notes were, but I made a mistake. I called the notes the wrong names. Then I figured, forget it, I'm not going to learn how to read music on it for a while, so I gave up and just dove into getting grooves going and figuring how to play that way.*
>
> *When I bought my Stick I wasn't able to communicate with Emmett a lot (this was way pre-email). So I figured this is what makes sense to me. This is the way I'll approach it. I'll have my right hand doing some chords and little lines to accompany the bass part, to really lock it in and make it solid and groove. Then I would see Emmett, maybe a couple of times a year. I remember playing for him and him saying, "I didn't really intend it to be played like that. You really showed me something new of a style*

that I really didn't think of or incorporate with it." I was very, very flattered by that, but at the same time I thought, "Well, what's the other way?" Then I'd watch him play and I'd go, "Oh, that makes total sense, that's great, that's genius-level playing there."

JR: *How was The Stick accepted in Vegas, back in the mid-seventies?*

DS: *Back then, it was really interesting. Effects pedals were the rage; there was a new one coming out each week. Synthesizers were being developed at a really fast rate. I can remember being on stage, and the keyboard player coming out with this new synthesizer and looking like a telephone operator. He had to plug these cables in and could only play one note at a time, and people thought that thing was cool. Then The Stick came out with all its potential and of course it was something new as well, so people were receptive to it. Everybody really liked it and came to see it, so I incorporated it as much as I could.*

I'd get a call to play bass and I would just show up with The Stick, pull that out first, and not really give them an opportunity to decide. I'd kind of force the hand and as long as it didn't get in the way, nobody really cared. Once they saw it, they'd say, "That thing is pretty cool."

I remember doing the Raquel Welch Show in Vegas. She really liked my Stick playing and said, "You know, we ought to feature that thing." She had a tune that she wrote, I think for her daughter, which was the chosen song to bring The Stick out. So I got this huge, 80ft cable and I walked out in front of the band and I got to play it. But then a couple of days later, I was told, "Don't come out in front of the band anymore." It was such an interesting looking instrument that it drew too much attention away from

Raquel. I kept playing The Stick but just kept that cable wrapped up around my feet. I couldn't unwind it and walk out anymore.

JR: *You moved to LA in 1977. What was the Stick community like in LA back then?*

DS: *Really small, really fun. I'd go to Emmett's a lot. Back then, Paul Edwards was at Stick Enterprises a lot too. He was a really good Stick player. He was in Kittyhawk. Along with Emmett, Kittyhawk was the big event that you'd go see, and Alphonso Johnson, and of course, Tony Levin.*

You'd play the little clubs, but I think everybody, at the same time, was trying to find a big opportunity like Tony Levin had, to go out and play and really showcase The Stick, and make it an integral part of something. That's what I was always looking for. People were playing in little clubs but I was always, for myself, just trying to get in a band or look for an opportunity to go, "Oh, I think this will work."

Back in the mid-seventies, bass player Tony Levin used to fool around between takes in the studio, often tapping relentlessly on his bass. When he was told about The Chapman Stick, an instrument created for just that kind of tapping, he was immediately curious, checked one out, and soon added a Stick to his instrumental arsenal.

"I have a memory of meeting Emmett a long time ago, when I had first heard about The Stick," says Levin. "I went to his place in LA to try it out, and I wasn't sure yet if I was going to get one. We talked about his ideas, and I'm not sure, but it seemed like he hadn't run into a guy like me, who was a bass player only, and played in rock bands on big stages in front of a lot of people. The issues I was interested in weren't really issues that he had thought about before. It was fun seeing him react and respond and then think, 'Oh yes, I could

135

do this and this...' You could almost see him address issues that hadn't really come up before with his playing of The Stick.

"The Stick was easy, very easy for me to adapt to because I'd been playing bass with a hammer-on technique for some time. In fact, when Emmett first started becoming known for playing The Stick, I didn't hear him, but within a few months, maybe 10 people I was either touring with or on record sessions with said, 'you know, there's this instrument, The Stick, that you should get because you play the bass the same way you play Stick, and it's going to be kind of the same thing.' I didn't know that not a lot of other people were playing it and I didn't really care. I had just heard that there was this instrument played with a hammer-on technique and I wanted to try it. I thought it could be very useful to me. When I first picked it up I just tried to play it like I had played the bass, with a hammer-on technique, and it wasn't a very big adjustment for me. Some of the aspects of it were, but actually playing a part, especially a bass part, was pretty simple for me. I've seen a lot of people pick up Sticks for the first time and try to play them and I think there's something very easy about the instrument and it's quite easy for some people. I've seen people just pick it up and play it.

"When I first got The Stick, the guy to listen to was Emmett. I never did reach his level of technical expertise, but I heard his approach to sound and I watched how he fingered things, so he was a big influence. In fact, I had to try in a way, on the early things, to get away from that way of playing Stick. I didn't get that far away, but I'd do parts with one finger on each hand rather than all four. But he's been a big influence on me and every Stick player, I'm sure."

Tony has become the most credited and arguably the most influential Stick player in the world. Like Schiff, Tony was a bass player before he became a Stick player and gravitated towards the lower end of the instrument. In his book, *Beyond the Bass Clef*, he writes, "I am attracted to The Stick's unique sound – it is strong, percussive, yet subtly different from the bass guitar sound... The tuning is unusual, I like that, too –it inspires me to come up with unusual lines."

Jim Reilly: *It was '76 when you first got The Stick?*

Tony Levin: *I'm not sure, that sounds right. I know I brought it to Peter Gabriel's first album, which was made in '76, so I certainly had it in '76.*

JR: *What was the first album you recorded Stick on?*

TL: *That's a good question. I know the artist. He's an old friend of mine, Gap Mangione. I was doing one of his solo albums[18]. It was brand new. In fact I had got The Stick only a day or two before that. It shows you what a kind guy he is that he let me take out this instrument that I could only play very simple parts on. But I actually did play it on a track on Gap's record.*

I took it to Peter Gabriel's first recording and the producer (Bob Ezrin) took one look at it and said, "Put that thing away."

Subsequent to that, I took it on tour with Peter and played it on one piece, a relatively simple piece, so I could start to get used to playing it on stage. The piece was called "Moribund of the Burgermeister" off Peter's first album. Even though I played bass on the album, I always performed that piece with Stick.

JR: *And it was on Peter's second album fairly prominently?*

TL: *Yeah, by then I was well under way with it. I treasured from the beginning the way it has a different kind of bass sound. The attack and just the nature of the different tunings made it*

---

[18] The album was titled *Gap Mangione*; A&M Records, SP-4621, released in 1976.

sound, in a subtle way, different than a bass. I thought, "This is something that is really appropriate for Peter Gabriel or some kind of alternative music."

Later, it's ironic that I played on so many albums that I began to be called for playing it on regular music, not just alternative, and it's fine for that too.

(Tony Levin with his first Stick.)

***JR:** What were some other initial reactions to The Stick back in the early days?*

TL: Producers were pretty scared by it. Engineers liked it because it has a good, clean sound. Especially down low, it's cleaner than a bass, clearer. But producers sometimes just aren't ready for something that looks really different, even if it sounds only a little different. But some did, and gosh knows how many albums over the years I used it on.

Here's a good example. Ironically, the same producer from that first Peter Gabriel album (Bob Ezrin), many years later, when I was playing on Pink Floyd's Momentary Lapse of Reason, *specifically asked me to bring The Stick and play it.*

The Stick found a home in Peter Gabriel's bands, especially during the seventies and eighties. "Peter always likes alternative things in all ways," says Tony. "He likes alternative music and he likes me to take alternative approaches to his music, so he's been a fan of The Stick since I first brought it out. He liked everything about it. Typical of Peter, he wanted to make things even more unusual, and one day, pretty early in our relationship, he looked at The Stick and said, 'What if you played that with thimbles on?' This must have been in the seventies. I said to him, 'It's different enough. I just want to make sure that it's in the right place and I'm not ready to take it to a place where it's even *more* different.' Frankly, I'm a little embarrassed that after all these years I still haven't tried playing it with thimbles. Together, we've enjoyed The Stick on a lot of Peter's music over the years. It's been one of the distinctive sounds about quite a few of his pieces. It became kind of a signature sound of the band in that era of Peter's music.

"I not only have played The Stick on a lot of albums, but I also write on it and some of my solo music, which is very important to me, has come from parts that I could never have played on any other instrument and I wouldn't have wanted to. The Stick would inspire certain sections of songs. I find it a very useful tool for being creative."

Tony has become one of the most sought after bassists/Stickists in the world. Listing his credits would take a book unto itself. Listing the number of Stick players who started playing Stick after seeing Tony perform with Peter Gabriel or King Crimson would take a book just as long.

Don Schiff worked in Vegas, Tony Levin travelled the world's stages, Kittyhawk sought that big break in the Los Angeles music scene. Paul Edwards saw Emmett perform back in The Electric Stick days, back in '73, at a small club in West Los Angeles. Edwards was a guitar player and slated to play at that same club, later in the evening. He had arrived early to "check out the competition." When Emmett walked on stage, the bizarre contraption Emmett was pulling out of its case instantly took Paul aback. This would have been Electric Stick number three: the prototype between the ebony board with the suspended pickup and the Stick with the pickup mounted under the strings.

Paul wrote about seeing Emmett in an article simply titled "The Stick," published in *Musician's Guide*, August 1976. He writes about the stunned look on people's faces when Emmett pulled out The Stick. He writes that when Emmett began to play, "the magic started to happen." And continues, "The sounds trembled over us; many harmonies, colors, and moods filled the room." He wrote about meeting Emmett after the show and knowing that "we had witnessed a new musical instrument of major proportions."

He wouldn't personally connect with The Stick until a couple of years later, after reading the *Guitar Player* article and seeing Emmett perform a second time. Kittyhawk formed a couple of years later, driven not by one Stick, but by two. Paul Edwards and fellow Stick player Daniel Bortz joined forces to bring The Stick to the world, and the world to The Stick.

Kittyhawk had success on a national level. Jim Schwartz wrote in *Guitar Player*, "Occasionally, a new musical group emerges which not only captures an audience's attention with its special sound, but also with the particular instruments that produce it. Kittyhawk is just such a group." A review in *Variety* stated, "Ensemble playing is particularly clean and tight, full of soaring solos and shifting moods. All-original instrumentals, many from a debut EMI America release, show enough variation in content to maintain interest and excite, especially when Bortz and Edwards are together on stick guitars [sic], hopping about as though on pogo sticks."

Alphonso Johnson was playing in Joe Zawinul's band Weather Report back in the early seventies, when Joe bought one of the first Sticks, but it wasn't Zawinul who introduced Johnson to The Stick. Emmett had seen Weather Report perform and thought Johnson "seemed to be playing lead bass lines as a front man on stage." Emmett thought The Stick would be perfect for the role Alphonso was playing, but did not pursue the matter. A year or so later, Johnson phoned Emmett out of the blue and ordered a Stick for himself.

It wasn't totally out of the blue for Johnson though. "I'll never forget that day that I was walking down Santa Monica Boulevard and I heard this sound coming out of this restaurant," Johnson says. "I went up the stairs, got to the top and looked around. Way back in the corner of the room, I saw Emmett and this percussionist playing. It sounded so incredible and I was so inspired that I contacted him shortly after that and got my first Stick. I was really curious about how he got all those sounds out of one instrument, and I liked the sound of solo Stick with percussion. To me it sounded so complete.

(Alphonso Johnson and his first Stick.)

"I didn't play my first Stick for almost two months," he continues. "I just sat it in the corner so I could look at it, and every day I'd walk by and try and figure out what I was going to do with it. Finally, I started taking lessons from Emmett. There I was, studying with the guy who invented the instrument; I thought that was a big deal.

"For me, what was great was that it took me back to basics. I had to learn all the stuff that I already knew how to do on bass all over again on Stick. Any instrument that you're going to master, or hopefully master, you're going to have to humble yourself and start at the beginning. You have to build a strong foundation in order to play."

Emmett wrote about other early Stick pioneers in his article "There Are Others," published in *Music America*, May 1977. Bart Carette of Brussels, Belgium was adapting classical guitar pieces by Bach, Segovia and others. Guitar player Jamie Glaser, from Boston, was playing jazz-rock lead lines on Stick with his band The Yarbles. Don Tavel applied his expertise in electronic music to The Stick, approaching the instrument as a "touch-controlled sound generator, to be interfaced with synthesizers, computers and Don's own electronic inventions."

David Torres, John Mahoney, Russell Tuttle, Herb Mickman, Don Baird and many, many more, were worthy of special attention. Some have since drifted away from The Stick. Others, like Bob Culbertson and Jim Bruno (who were the first qualified Stick instructors in the San Francisco Bay area), Don Schiff, Tony Levin and Alphonso Johnson continue to explore The Stick and Emmett's two-handed technique and continue inspiring musicians to pick up the instrument.

Emmett taught most of the early Stick players and led the way, in terms of musical ideas and adventurous explorations. Soon however, the Stick students started giving back to Emmett as much as he had given them. They showed Emmett music and showed him directions he had never thought of for The Stick. Emmett reinforces Don Schiff's story in which Don had come for a lesson and ended up showing him funk rhythms made up of bass and chord riffs polyphonically tapped between two hands. Emmett felt like he was the student.

Feedback from players was often more than musical. Drawing both from his own experiences playing and others' wish lists, Emmett continued refining and modifying The Stick. Through the seventies The Stick got wider; the pitch of the strings was raised a whole tone; large 'jumbo' frets replaced the regular guitar frets; an S-shaped sheet metal belt hook replaced the wooden one; a black anodized sheet metal, height-adjustable pickup housing replaced the wooden housing; and a pair of rigid, spring-tempered steel trusses were inlayed along the rear of the neck for added strength and rigidity. The Stick as an instrument, along with Emmett's music, was always in constant motion, always searching, always being refined.

While Stick players were busy creating their own music, Emmett and Yuta were hard at work creating Stick Enterprises. Stick Enterprises' goals were simple: manufacture, promote, and sell The Stick, promote Emmett's music, and educate people on Emmett's technique. Patents were granted and trademarks registered. All this operated from the Chapman's Laurel Canyon home. The business end fell to Yuta. She kept the books, took orders, handled customer service, organized social events at the Chapman's house and other places and booked Emmett's tours. She was really active and a lot of it was tedious, hard work, especially getting gigs for Emmett and handling music store sales.

"She was the one that really got a lot of things going," says Emmett. "She wanted to keep up with the pack in a business way, make sure all the obligations were met, and all the correspondences were done, much more so than I did at the time." Emmett headed production, but Yuta made sure that The Sticks found their way out of the shop and into the eagerly awaiting hands of new Stick players around the world. Without Yuta it's easy to believe that Emmett would have remained the only Stick Player.

Business was hard and money wasn't plentiful. When money would come in, Emmett was in the habit of sending it right back out again on supplies or necessary Stick components. The Volkswagen Beetle they bought when first starting out was traded for an order of Stick pickups. Later, Emmett and Yuta had the choice to buy the property beside theirs on Yucca Trail or place the first Stick advertisement in *Guitar Player*. They chose the ad. It ran in the September 1976 issue on page 66. It read, "TAP SOFTLY AND CARRY A BIG ORCHESTRA" and listed the music stores where Sticks were available at the time (Sam Ash Stores – New York, E. U. Wurlitzer – Boston, Coast Music – Orange County, WPM Whitter Plaza Music – LA, Guitar Showcase – San Jose, Gray Gand Music – Chicago, Reliable Music – Charlotte, N.C.). The 'Stickman' logo—a caricature of Emmett with elongated, spider-like fingers tapping a Stick—created by brother Dan, runs down the ad's right side.

Emmett began writing about his technique and The Stick. *Musician's Guide* published some of his articles. In the March 1976 issue, in an article titled "Complimenting Your Sound," Emmett goes through the list of effects he used at the time to modify his basic Stick sound. He also lends some insight into his approach to creating music and trying to get at the ever-elusive sound in his head:

I play The Stick, and I identify with both jazz saxophonists and rock lead guitarists. I've spent years going after the sound I heard inside, going through various combinations of effects equipment, amps and speakers, string experiments. What I have now gets me closer than I've ever been to that sound inside. I start with the clean sound of The Stick, a sound somewhat like a harpsichord or clavichord with bass (somewhere between acoustic and electric)...

Working off the natural Stick string sound, I add just the basic ingredients—wah, fuzz, phase shift, and echo. This is all I personally need for expression...

What am I still looking for? Sounds and ideas from other musicians in collaboration on lead and percussion instruments! When I go on tour to play concerts and music store clinics, I look for musicians who have unusual musicianship and a distinctive sound.

In Charlotte, North Carolina, Emmett found Cannonball LeClure on E-flat soprano sax and in Bloomington, drummer Peter Erskine fit the bill. Keshavan Maslak on reeds and Abdul Shahid on drums played with Emmett in New York. Jamie Glaser joined him on guitar in Boston.

"Stick-Bass in Fifths, A New Language," by Emmett in the February 1976 *Musician's Guide*, made the case for turning the standard bass tuning upside down and exploring the relationship of notes in the lower register by intervals of a fifth rather than the more conventional bass tuned in fourths. He writes:

It's a trade-off. Bass in fourths makes scales easier. In fifths, wide intervallic leaps are better for the fingers. Percussively speaking, a sequence of strings in fifths provides the equivalents of bass drum, toms, snare, bells and cymbals.

When I experimentally go back to bass tuned in fourths, I feel boxed in, committed to conventional bass licks, scales and pentatonic scales. The language becomes too much like my melodic side, the left hand copying the right...

Creative advance won't come from copying lead instruments. The source is deeper inside the physics of the bass register, and deeper into what my ear listens for.

(Emmett and Peter Erskine in Bloomington.)

Accolades for both Emmett's music and The Stick rolled in. Don Tavel wrote a glowing article in *Music America*, in December 1976, titled "The Ultimate Compositional Instrument: The Stick." At the time Tavel was serving as the Assistant Director of the Indiana University Center for Electronic and Computer Music.

He writes:

If it were possible to accommodate the needs of the composer without sacrifice, an instrument would have to be made with no less than a five-octave range to cover the most commonly used registers. It should be able to be played orchestrally, with both hands providing up to ten individually controlled and selected notes simultaneously. It must be capable of subtleties usually associated with the most expressive of instruments. Perhaps most important, it must have a clear and logical tuning system which allows the composer to utilize desired musical materials in any register, position, or configuration chosen. Furthermore, this instrument should be capable of different sound qualities simultaneously (a feat not possible with any traditional instrument this author knows of).

Strangely enough, such an instrument exists. I am referring to the Chapman Electric Stick Touchboard brought into existence through the dedication and insight of its incredible inventor, Emmett Chapman...

In their annual music issue, *Playboy* magazine named The Chapman Stick the "Musical Toy of the Year" for 1976. "The Stick, by Emmett Chapman, looks like a bodyless [sic] guitar but plays more like a piano," the article reads. In the same issue, *Playboy* named *Red Octopus* by Jefferson Starship the best pop/rock L.P. and *That's The Way of the World* by Earth, Wind and Fire won for best rhythm-and-blues. The top jazz album, according to *Playboy*, was the Chick Corea's album *No Mystery*, featuring Corea, Stanley Clarke, Lenny White and Al Di Meola. Honours in the Readers Poll went to Elton John, Eric Clapton, Who drummer Keith Moon and Paul McCartney, who won in the best bass player category. *Playboy* readers named The Eagles best group.

By the end of 1976, Emmett had made 220 Sticks. He built the first 10 by himself, almost entirely by hand. Soon being the sole performer, teacher, businessman and builder became too much and he began subcontracting some of the production work.

Emmett did hundreds of shows throughout the seventies. It seems like he would play anywhere, do whatever he needed to do to get his music heard. One time he was late for an open stage gig at the Whisky a Go Go. He raced up to the front of the club in his Volkswagen Beetle, jumped out, and flew into the venue. He arrived just as he was supposed to go on stage. He pulled his Stick out, fumbled with plugging into an unfamiliar amplifier, played his tunes, packed up and left the club. Outside he found the door of his Beetle still wide open with the engine running, waiting for him right where he had left it.

The 1970s were about beginnings. The Stick, hundreds of Stick players and Stick Enterprises itself, all took their first steps. The Stick was born through the explorative, freethinking ideals of the sixties but didn't get lost when those cultural ideals shifted away from the main stage. Through the artist, through music, The Stick would inevitably end up in the hands of people who would see it for what it was: a new way for musicians to tap into the sounds in their heads and show the world the possibilities when a brand new instrument with its own unique performing method combine in the hands of gifted artists.

Chapter 10 – Finding Voices

"I started out playing it thinking, 'Oh boy, I can play with my right hand (EMMETT PLAYS), and I can play drum-like and rhythmically.' (HE PLAYS SOME MORE) The next thought was that I'd play some chords that I already know (AND AGAIN) and start doing that. I could do it right away. That was back in 1969. I didn't know I was going to spend five years developing the instrument before I started manufacturing it.

"After that, I began to get into the bass and I added a bass string and then another bass string to get way down into the bass register and started playing bass lines. I didn't know I was going to do that. At first I didn't have any wish to do that. It just naturally developed.

"Then in these last two years, I'm swallowing up the drums. I've gotten so ambitious playing driving rhythms and keeping the rhythm going. I'll practice that for hours, just rhythms going with my left hand and independent rhythms with my right hand, going through all the chord changes that I'd normally practice, but doing it with different rhythms.

"So it's percussion, it's like drums, it's like bass, it's like guitar and it's like keyboard. It's these four main major instruments and the techniques of all those are on this one instrument."

-Emmett responding to questions, Sam Ash Clinic, September 11, 1984

The Chapman Stick was born in the sixties, took its first steps in the seventies, and entered into the eighties with style. In 1980, you could buy a ten-string Chapman Stick complete with case, stereo cord and

Emmett's instruction book *Free Hands,* for $750. California residents added 6 per cent state sales tax.

In 1980, Jeff Beck bought one of those $750 Sticks (with case, cord and book). Actually, Beck's manager bought it for him as a birthday present. Jeff had seen "this guy playing it in a club who he thought had invented it." He mentioned the Stick sighting to his manger and voila: "Sticks make good birthday presents." The October 16, 1980 edition of *Rolling Stone* magazine featured a great picture of Mr. Beck tapping his Stick. In the picture, his left hand looks pretty good, grabbing his Stick like he would a guitar, with his thumb providing support from behind the instrument's neck. His right hand technique looks a little rough. His thumb is way out in front, floating above The Stick. He should be supporting his right hand with the thumb resting on the bass side's bevelled edge and the fingers reaching over, tapping the melody strings. He wouldn't have had enough support in his right hand to do really fast single-note runs and he would end up with control issues too, if he wasn't careful. All in all though, Jeff looked pretty comfortable with his new toy.

As usual, Emmett was busy. He published his method book: *Free Hands, A New Discipline of Fingers on Strings: Basic Techniques for Playing The Chapman Stick Touchboard®, a Stringed Instrument.* For years, Emmett would write up lessons for his growing number of Stick students. Gradually, the lessons piled up. Emmett gathered some of his best, and along with articles he had written for *Musician's Guide, Musician, Player and Listener* and *Music America,* he published them under the collective title *Free Hands.* 'Free Hands' was Emmett's goal and the enticement for other Stick players, new and old alike. Jim Schwartz reviewed *Free Hands* for *Guitar Player:* "While specifically written as a sourcebook for Stick players,

Chapman's well-executed, 78-page text is also loaded with substantive music theory—all pertaining to mastering his creation...*Free Hands* just might be your ticket for sampling some of what The Stick has to offer the musician looking for different sounds."

(Emmett leading a Stick seminar.)

The concert, performance and seminar schedule didn't slow down. With Yuta still booking gigs and Emmett still delivering the goods, praise like the following from Barry Goldberg, commissioner of cultural affairs at UCLA, flowed in:

February 27, 1980

Emmett Chapman:

Thank you very much for your performance in the Kerckhoff Coffee House on February 19, 1980. Everyone that was present enjoyed your program very much. I must echo Daily Bruin *writer*

Chris Hoard that your show was "educational as well as entertaining." I am looking forward to arranging another UCLA show for you because the response was so enthusiastic. I sincerely recommend that all colleges and universities consider a date featuring "The Stick." If any college rep would like to find out the college audience reaction, I would be more than happy to serve as a reference.

Thank you,

Barry Goldberg

P.S. Thank your wife for the excellent arrangements.

And this from Dana Krempels at the University of Southern California:

May 25, 1980

Dear Mr. Chapman:

The school year is nearly over, and I want to thank you once more for your two wonderful performances at the USC CoffeeHouse. Whether the publicity is short-notice or long-term, you always fill the house with quiet, attentive and very appreciative music lovers, who do not stir until the last note has sounded.

This is not surprising. You and The Stick are such a smooth and unique team, that even the uninitiated are instantly enthralled by the incredible and beautiful sounds you make together. Your music is unlike anything they have ever heard!

You have always been a pleasure, and your lovely Mrs. Chapman has always been helpful and kind. I hope that your performances mark the anniversary of a long and happy association between Emmett Chapman and The Stick and the USC CoffeeHouse.

Best of luck in all.

Sincerely,

Dana Krempels

USC CoffeeHouse Chairman

And while the 1980s started with so much forward momentum for Emmett and The Stick, it was in 1981 that things really took off. It started as a little riff – a couple of notes bouncing back and forth between two fingers. Quickly the riff got louder and faster, eventually turning into a whirling, pulsing trill. Suddenly, abruptly, a deep, percussive bass note cut the trill short and a heavy, funk-rich groove broke out. The groove continued, establishing itself till a backward sounding cymbal cut through, signalling the rest of the band to join in. The song was "Elephant Talk," the band King Crimson, the album, *Discipline.* That funky, whirling, polyrhythmic Stick riff that Tony Levin came up with to introduce the song, was the Stick riff heard around the world. Of course, not too many people realized that it was a Stick that fired the shot. Most people chalked the riff up to one of Crimson's two guitar players, Robert Fripp or Adrian Belew.

"I don't remember too much about the writing of the song," Levin says, "but I do remember that at some time I chirped up, in a way that I usually don't, and said that I had a really good line and suggested that I start the song. Just the sound of that piece, which starts the album *Discipline,* that track starts off alone with the sound of The Stick and captures the listener's ear in a way that is kind of like, 'What is this? This isn't a guitar; this isn't something I've heard before.' I'm no expert about how people listen to things, but I've heard from a lot of younger Stick players that this is what they heard that got them interested in the Stick.

"Let me tell you something else about that line. Like many things I play, it's very easy to play, but only because I tuned one string down. I was just kind of fooling around, trying to find a line, and I tuned one string down a half step. In subsequent years I saw lots of Stick players say, 'Boy that line is really hard,' and I'd watch them try to play it without tuning it down. They were almost embarrassed for me when I'd show them how easy it is. It's just a two-finger line with the string tuned down. So there's kind of a simple trick to it that makes it very easy. It was never intended as a hard, technical thing."

More than anyone else, Tony showed The Chapman Stick to the world. He had owned a Stick since 1976 and had used it extensively with Peter Gabriel, but with King Crimson in the eighties, Tony had found the perfect group and the perfect vehicle for him to explore his relationship with The Stick. Crimson was pushing boundaries. On many of their most popular tracks from the trio of albums they recorded in the eighties – *Discipline*, *Beat* and *Three of a Perfect Pair* – Levin and his Stick provided the low end groove.

"For Crimson, an alternative band that looks to do things in different ways," Tony continues, "Stick was the perfect instrument. In 1981, on the *Discipline* album, something about the bass side of The Stick and the way you can jump around and be percussive like a drum, was a great way to respond to Bill Bruford's unusual approach to rock drumming that he was using in the eighties. We did three great albums that featured The Stick quite a bit."

Robert Fripp wrote in the diary he kept during the band rehearsals that would lead to the *Discipline* recordings: "Tony is mostly playing The Stick instead of the bass guitar, and with its attack it provides a tuned-percussion effect doubling BB's (Bill Bruford's) boo-bams. A beautiful sustained low end Tony found 'killed him.'"

King Crimson has always attracted exploring, adventurous musicians and listeners: people prone to taking risks. In 1981, on the *Discipline* album, Tony and The Stick were a perfect fit:

Jim Reilly: *Let's talk about the* Discipline *album. As a Stick album and as an album in general it seems to be landmark, not only for the four players who created it, but also for a lot of King Crimson fans and Stick players alike.*

Tony Levin: *I think* Discipline *was a breakthrough album in a number of ways, certainly with my era in King Crimson. That was our first album. In ways it was the best, and in ways it has influenced us ever since. Even though we're too progressive a band to go back and do more of that style, at least intentionally, we still want to have that kind of breakthrough on every album. And that's something you really can't even do intentionally, let alone every time. That's partly why King Crimson is such an intense band and being in it is such an intense experience.*

Having started out in '81 with Discipline, *we wanted to match that with a breakthrough album each time, and that creates a lot of pressure within the band. It was also for me, the first chance to really bring The Stick to the fore. In King Crimson, people pay more attention to the members of the band than they did with the Peter Gabriel band, so it was a good chance to bring The Stick out in front of people who were listening to progressive music. Especially on "Elephant Talk," where the piece started out on Stick. The Stick figure, which could have been somewhere in the background, became the main feature of the piece. It helped The Stick to become known. It was an interesting breakthrough in a few ways.*

JR: What did The Stick bring to that album that the bass didn't? Why did that end up becoming a Stick album rather than more of a bass album?

TL: It's hard to say. It's usual that with King Crimson I'm always looking for something new, something that I haven't done before, some breakthrough in my little niche of the Crimson world, which is the bass end of things. The Stick was it at that time.

Not just The Stick but I started playing much busier than I had before. Generally I think of myself as a simple player. I play the roots of things and hold things together, and I did do that to some extent with King Crimson. That was my first year playing with Bill Bruford, who is a very creative player and who plays very busy. He also plays a lot of cross-rhythms. Instead of trying to hold things down, literally and figuratively, with a big fat bass sound and a few notes, as I would have (actually that was my first inclination with all the new Crimson material for that album) I gradually, in rehearsal, thought I would experiment with things I had never done. Like going with Bill and maybe playing his part that's in 15/8, playing that with him with one hand and doing occasional 4/4 things with the other hand on the low notes.

Things like that are just the kinds of stuff that you do in that band. I've never stopped appreciating how lucky I've been to be in a band that is so creative that you can try out things like that.

King Crimson's music wasn't easily accessible to the masses and Levin's Stick work with Crimson didn't reach the public en masse, but it struck chords with the right people. Whereas Levin's Stick line in Peter Gabriel's "Shock the Monkey" was lost on listeners behind well-placed pop hooks and insightful, artfully delivered lyrics,

Crimson still lived on the fringes. In the eighties incarnation of King Crimson with Robert Fripp and Adrian Belew on guitar, Belew singing, Bill Bruford on drums and Tony switching between bass and Stick, The Stick was noticed by adventurous musicians. These were just the kind of people who would want to become Stick players themselves.

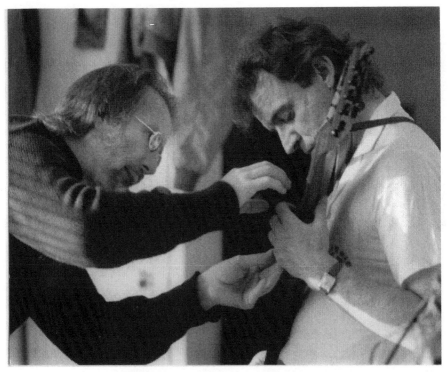

(Jack Bruce receiving private instruction. Photo by Dan Chapman)

Levin wasn't the only one releasing important Stick albums in the early part of the decade. Along with *Discipline*, Stick Enterprises mentioned three others in their December 1981 newsletter:

"Brian Dorr of Albuquerque, New Mexico, has just produced his first album, Fire Stick *featuring The Stick in solo, duo, and*

trio on standards and his originals. His variety of techniques, effects and instrumentation is instructive and provocative.

"Kittyhawk, the LA jazz-rock quartet with Paul Edwards on The Stick and vocals, Dan Bortz on The Stick, guitar (fretless and fretted), and cello, and guest artist Randy Strom on The Stick, has now recorded their second album, Race for the Oasis, released by Capitol and EMI America. The Stick is extensively involved in the band's compositions, arrangements, and solos.

"Alphonso Johnson's Spellbound, recently released by Epic, features The Stick on the front cover and throughout the music, and sometimes in solo. Alphonso, although he is a bass player, has used The Stick as a primary tool of composition on the album, as on the past three of his albums."

(John Entwistle and his Stick.)

Emmett was also busy preparing his music for wide scale release. For years, Emmett had been giving solo performances and having musicians sit in with him on gigs. Now he was settling into regular gigs around LA with well-known saxophonist and multi-instrumentalist Ray Pizzi, and drummer Bruce Gary. Gary had had hit recordings with the pop rock group The Knack and would join Emmett in the studio to record the culmination of Emmett's musical searching: an album he titled *Parallel Galaxy*. Throughout his musical career, Emmett had held off from presenting his own music on recordings. He was content to present himself and The Stick live, in person, in intimate settings where people could both see and hear what he was doing. He liked the intimacy with his audience and valued the chances for musicians to ask questions after a show and maybe even tap a few notes for themselves. But that was about to change. Emmett was ready, his chops were in top form, and the music coming through his hands was sounding like the music in his head. He was about to share the sounds he heard in his own parallel galaxy with the world.

The songs that made up *Parallel Galaxy* were worked in slowly over the years. Emmett had played most of them solo, often breaking them down in seminars, explaining the left and the right hand parts and how those two sides related to each other: chords in the left, melody in the right, counterpoint, polyrhythms – it was all there. Emmett's music had always been unique and complex. He was striving for a complete music. The two hands supported and reinforced each other but they also stood up on their own, like two completely separate musicians, each following his own score. It's as if he was trying to create a situation in which the left and right sides of his brain were in equal opposition: the intuitive, artistic side, fully developed, existing in perfect (sometimes dissonant, almost always complex and extended) harmony with the logical, precise, mathematical side. *Parallel Galaxy* showed Emmett's music as new, unique, diverse, and challenging for the more casual listener, much like the man himself. But it was all there. It was as if the boy playing accordion in church had met Coltrane, Tyner, John McLaughlin, Jimi Hendrix, Debussy, Stravinsky, even a bit of Bartok and they all took a journey on a brand new musical instrument. The album was not only Emmett's showcase but it also featured blues and country-style harmonica from brother Dan, driving rock rhythms from Gary and vocal gymnastics from Josh Hanna. Emmett was a fan of Hanna's, whose vocal adventures at the time were in the same experimental vein as Tim Buckley's, albeit with far more control and refinement.

The press release below accompanied Emmett's recording:

Information about Parallel Galaxy

By Emmett Chapman

This is my first record, recorded live and with no overdubbing in my four-track home studio.

I chose simple duo and solo formats on all cuts in order to clearly present the core ideas of my music.

There are ten songs, six of them originals. I play my stringed and fretted invention, The Stick®, on all songs, including four with vocalist Josh Hanna, two with drummer Bruce Gary, one with my brother Dan on harmonicas, and three in solo.

Josh is primarily a solo artist who can mesmerize an audience with his instrumental and percussive vocalizations, jazz arrangements, and originals. He sings an incredible range of moods, rhythms, and textures through his customized rack of electronic effects.

Bruce frequently tours all over the world playing drums for Bob Dylan, Jack Bruce and formerly for The Knack. Bruce and I have played in duo at many clubs and colleges over the years.

Dan is a freelance graphic artist in the LA entertainment industries. He did the design and photography for the Galaxy jacket. He has a bag of well broken in harmonicas, dating back to his junior high school days.

I recorded this album on a four-track, quarter-inch Tascam model 34. I mixed down and edited on my Teac A-3300 SX half-rack, quarter inch machine. My board is a Tascam model M-30. The monitor playback is a Yamaha middle-of-the-line stereo set.

The Stick was recorded direct through the board with no miking, and I played the monitor system as if it were my live sound equipment. The Stick is a stereo, ten-stringed instrument with two groups of strings, five melody strings tuned in descending fourth intervals, and five bass-and-chord strings in ascending fifth intervals. There is a separate pickup for each group.

I plug The Stick into my pedal board, which currently has chorus, phasing, flanging, limiting, fuzz, and echo.

Also on the pedal board is Patch of Shades, ™ which I manufacture. It controls some of these other effects, and crossfades from the straight Stick melody sound into any combination of effects by foot pressure on the pad. It also fades into a built-in wah. Roughly half of my sound is processed but I'm always fading back to the plain sound of Stick strings.

On the record there is much new material – six original songs, three unrecorded musicians, a relatively new instrument, some newly discovered music theory, and lots of improvisation of the unpredictable sort. Even the production process was unusual in being so minimal.

And so I'd like to share with you some of the ideas that went into each song:

SIDE 1

Back Yard (by Emmett) – I structured this song around familiar 'down home' chord changes, which are gradually stretched out along the circle of fourths to include neighbouring chords, then stretched further to tie in more remote chords. My brother Dan plays blues harmonica lines against my interwoven 'fingerpicking' arrangements, a special ten-fingered Stick technique. Dan plays F and A-flat harmonicas for this song in the key of C.

Margueritas in the Waves (by Emmett) – I taped down the strings at the bridge for most of this solo. It reminded me of a one-man mariachi band, and so one summer day at Malibu, while laughing at the huge waves battering me around (and also swallowing a good deal of ocean), I thought of the title and the dizzy 'Margueritas' theme.

Eleanor Rigby (by Lennon and McCartney) – A very strange encounter with this Beatles standard. Eight-tone diminished scales coexist with whole-tone scales. Josh had a hand in the arrangement as well, resurrecting hosts of tormented lost souls.

Pumpernickel Pump (by Emmett) – Old Thirties hot licks here, but with chords moving backwards from the usual fourths *progressions of that decade. The shuffle with Bruce felt like an old-time dance step, which I dubbed the 'Pumpernickel Pump.'*

Waltzing Matilda - Matilda has never been taken to the Outback before, and it didn't turn out to be a 'waltz.' Instead there's a martial atmosphere, with Josh vocalizing fife and drum effects through his electronics rack. I play some unusual harmonic twists to the theme. Of course, Josh takes it somewhere else, summoning forth a very hyper Aborigine. He follows this with a stalwart rendition of the lyrics.

SIDE 2

A Lotus on Irish Streams (by John McLaughlin) – This was one of my very first song arrangements on The Stick. The song is by my favourite musician, John McLaughlin. On this solo rendition I concentrate on the acoustic characteristics of this electric instrument, using subtle fingering effects, dynamics and embellishments.

Voices (by Josh Hanna and Emmett) – Josh and I totally improvised this performance, with no forethought or preparation except that I 'treated' The Stick with masking tape by the bridge to mute the sound. Josh sang into his kalimba and discovered 'voices' inside.

My Favorite Things (music by Richard Rodgers) – My arrangement of this sedate Sound of Music *tune was inspired by an entirely different source, John Coltrane and his rampaging quartet of the early Sixties. I've been trying to recreate the magic of that arrangement ever since I built my first Stick instrument in 1969, and even as early as 1962 when I played guitar and first heard that* Africa/Brass *album. Bruce and I play on the polyrhythms of twelve, weaving in and out of two sixes, four threes and three fours.*

Parallel Galaxy (by Emmett) – This is my latest fantasy in music theory, and is based entirely on my 'offset modal wheel' depicted on the album jacket. Although the recorded theme is simple, the musical discoveries are far-reaching and unify into one twelve-spoke system, the chords and scales that have been used, more or less intuitively, by classical and jazz composers. Having gotten clues from some close correspondences between music and astrology, it was like discovering a galaxy similar to ours, but where one or two basic physical laws have been shifted. An 'Earth' in such a galaxy might be unstable and dualistic – a Paradise that can fluctuate and change into a state of falseness and treachery (the altered chemistry of 'forbidden fruit'). Josh again reaches into his imagination and conjures up an Alien Being who travels on the wind of stars.

Gypsy (by Emmett) – Here is my solo space for some independent, two-handed rhythm playing – melody against bass. It's a completely different way of improvising, and is my newest discovery on strings. In the past, I've tried to incorporate the skills of piano, bass, and guitar into The Stick method, and now drums are creeping in! This song's harmonic structure is inspired from ancient Gypsy music, and I like the free feeling of phrasing right-hand modal melodies against the steady rhythm-chords of the left hand.

Here's hoping my passion will become your pastime.

Emmett Chapman

Los Angeles, California

June 1, 1985

There were actually three studio versions of *Parallel Galaxy*. One was even recorded at Chick Corea's Mad Hatter recording studio. But it was the third version, the one Emmett recorded in his home studio on Yucca Trail (workshop, family home, Stick Enterprises and now recording studio) that had the right vibe – that right mix of innocence and confidence, which hit the mark. Emmett was finally ready to stand back and present a permanent record of his music to the world: the music that had compelled him to create an entirely new musical instrument to express the sounds in his head.

Jazztimes reviewer A. David Franklin wrote: "The tunes showcase Chapman's technical wizardry on his invention, but irrespective of that, constitute a nicely balanced program of very listenable music. The stylistic variety, instrumental virtuosity, and excellence of sound quality make this record a superior first release."

Adam Ward Seligman wrote in *Jazziz* magazine: "The true importance of this record is in introducing The Stick both as a solo voice and as a compositional tool. Does it work? It does and extremely well. Chapman is a skilled player and his Stick alternately burns with fire, and soothes with ice as he taps his way through both his original songs, which make up the bulk of the album, and the covers, which include "A Lotus on Irish Streams." "Lotus," which was written for guitar, piano and violin, sounds as full as the Mahavishnu version and even goes beyond, with some added flurries of notes on the melody strings."

"There's nothing calculated or insincere on the entire album; the overall feeling is one of solid musicianship and quiet inspiration," wrote Bill Tilland in *Option* magazine. "A first album of this calibre is rare, and it really doesn't matter how much credit should go to

Chapman the musician, and how much to Chapman the inventor. Either way, he (and the listener) can't lose."

The *Parallel Galaxy* band, Emmett, Josh Hanna, Bruce Gary and brother Dan, would also perform their tunes live. Randy Heddon reviewed a show at Donte's in North Hollywood for *Music Connection*: "You get the feeling from Chapman of a man true to his musical ideals, who has succeeded in his own way, without compromise – something too rarely seen. Even if Chapman's music isn't exactly your genre, the chance to see the incredible Stick in the hands of the master is an experience not to be missed."

While accolades and encouraging reviews rolled in, trouble was just around the corner. Ever since Emmett discovered his two-handed tapping technique, there were always three forces at play: technique, instrument and music. With Emmett, all three forces lived outside of the mainstream. In 1985, 26 year-old guitarist Stanley Jordan released his debut album titled *Magic Touch*. It was produced by guitar virtuoso Al Di Meola and featured an all-star cast of session players including Charnett Moffett, Peter Erskine and Omar Hakim. The mass music press loved it and gave Jordan's first recording rave reviews. Jordan's playing was instantly accessible and easily fit in the jazz section of the local record store. *Magic Touch* was a runaway success. It charted number one on *Billboard* magazine's jazz chart for 51 weeks, garnered two Grammy nominations and was certified Gold in the U.S. and Japan.

Jordan's unique twist on guitar virtuosity was two-handed tapping. He tapped the strings against the frets with both hands approaching the fretboard from opposite sides and at 90-degree angles, just like Emmett, but he did it on a regular electric guitar.

Jordan had modified his instrument like Emmett had done years earlier. He too dropped his guitar's action as low as possible, re-tuned his instrument entirely in fourth intervals and put a damper at the headstock end of the fretboard to prevent the string from sounding when he lifted his fingers off. All of these were the same modifications Emmett had made on The Freedom Guitar and had carried over to The Stick.

The press had a much easier time explaining what Stanley Jordan was doing with his two-handed tapping technique. They only had one thing to explain, one thing to justify. It was an easier sell. In Emmett's case, the instrument struck people first. This needed explaining. Then the music, which was a fusion of jazz, classical, new age, rock and blues didn't fit nicely into any one category. It needed rationalizing. Then, if there were still space, Emmett's technique would receive some mention. But none, or at least very few, in the mainstream press had caught onto the fact that Emmett's driving force was his technique and it had been driving the creation of the instrument from the absolute beginning.

With Jordan, all that needed explaining was his technique. Everyone understood the guitar. The songs on *Magic Touch*, even Stanley's original compositions, were unquestionably jazz tunes. The only thing that needed clarification was how Jordan was able to get so much sound out of one guitar, and that was easy to explain. The press just said he "played guitar like a piano by tapping the strings with both hands." There was no need to go into how the angle of the right hand shifted to line up with the strings making fast runs much easier than they would be if one kept their hands in a more traditional position. There was no need to go into modifying the instrument or extending ranges or retuning. All that the press needed Jordan to explain was his technique and that technique became the selling point for the marketers and promoters. The problem arose when many in the mainstream music industry went one step further and ignored Emmett's role in developing the two-handed tapping technique and placed full credit on Stanley Jordan's shoulders.

Jordan acknowledged Emmett and other guitar players like Jimmy Webster and Lenny Breau, who also tapped on their guitars, but said that he discovered and developed the technique independently. In a June 23rd, 1985 *Los Angeles Times* article written by Leonard Feather, Emmett claims that Jordan was well aware of his music and The Stick. "I met Jordan in 1977," Chapman recalls in the article, "at a music-store clinic held in the San Jose area. A year earlier, a friend of mine did a Stick clinic at the same store and spent some time with Stanley. He was interested in the instrument and I thought he was going to get one, but I guess somewhere along the way he decided not to." In 1982 Emmett and Stanley exchanged letters and sent each other tapes of their music. Emmett sent Stanley a copy of the *Free Hands* method book. Jordan expressed interest in buying a Stick and Emmett offered a significant discount on the list price, but Jordan never did take him up on his offer.

In a 1985 *Guitar Player* interview (later reprinted in the book *New Directions in Modern Guitar,* 1986), Jim Ferguson asked Jordan, "Why don't you use The Chapman Stick?" Jordan replied: "I like the Stick; I'm sure that I'll be getting one, but I don't have time to learn it right now." Jordan liked the voicing potential of The Stick's 10 strings, but thought that the setup and tuning was too foreign to him. He said that he preferred the thicker strings, the shorter scale length and the sound of his own guitar, when compared to The Stick.

Both Stanley and Emmett had their own approach to two-handed tapping with marvellous, musically rich results. The two are closely related in their technique; they are both tapping on stringed and fretted musical instruments in very similar styles. Their style differs from the way almost every other string tapper had played before. However, they are playing different instruments. Jordan found all the sounds he needed on guitar. Emmett needed more. He needed a wider sonic range, the notes of both a bass and a guitar. Emmett discovered his technique independently on a modified guitar and then created an instrument to fully explore the technique. Jordan discovered the technique on a standard electric guitar and modified it to better facilitate the technique. Jordan says he started exploring his two-handed technique in 1976. Emmett discovered his in 1969.

Both musicians made (and continue to make) engaging music. Unfortunately, the media placed one above the other, rather than side-by-side as two independent musicians both exploring their own paths. Why didn't Stanley Jordan play a Stick? He didn't have the need. He got all the sound he required out of the guitar; it felt right in his hands. There really shouldn't have been an issue and it's unfortunate that an overzealous music and entertainment business created one.

Under mounting pressure to set the record straight, in July 1986, Emmett published an article titled: "Two Hands across the Board: documenting the new method of playing strings." He felt like it was time to speak up on behalf of his own work:

The two-handed tapping technique has opened up wide, new territory for guitar, and will see decades of tremendous growth. It's not just a fad, as some might believe.

The guitars will become more elaborate, because this eight-fingered tapping method just cries out for more strings on the fretboard—eight, ten strings, a wider board, a longer board. And also, this technique is just waiting to happen on the guitar synthesizer.

The guitar industry as a whole, including the guitar magazines, and the recording, entertainment and manufacturing entities, will encourage each innovative tapping guitarist to credit another guitarist, as they are doing now—the Eddie Van Halen, the Stanley Jordan school, and so on.

Meanwhile The Stick, which has been here in full form all along, gets shunted aside, even as guitars become more and more like The Stick. My innovations over years of playing this technique and manufacturing this instrument are now being adapted to guitar—the ultra-low action, the very close pickup adjustment, the uniform fourths tuning, the string damper by the nut. The guitar, as it gradually changes, will no doubt take on further Stick-like characteristics—perhaps a more vertical playing position, or dual string sections on one board, or a totally rectangular board with no arch and no taper.

And all of the many inspired Stick players, who have spent some years performing and teaching this technique, are left out of the big picture as the major publicity is diverted exclusively to tapping guitarists.

So it must be time for me to speak up on behalf of my own work, and to tell it like it is. The guitar media and industry, if faced with the contradiction, can't forever ignore what really happened...

Emmett then described the August evening in 1969 when, while under the spell of Jimi Hendrix, he first began tapping on his modified guitar. He writes about the evolution from guitar to Stick, always guided by his unique two-handed tapping method. And he continues, describing the difference between his technique and the tapping that most guitar players had done in the past and were doing at the time.

He concluded his six-page article with:

My work has been long lasting and has proven fruitful and productive for many musicians. It is well known throughout the industry and the media. Over the past eleven years, Stick Enterprises has given out 250,000 Stick brochures describing the two-handed tapping method in detail. These brochures, along with many thousands of accompanying recorded and printed materials, have been given to individual musicians, music stores worldwide, and have been available at most of the U.S. music trade shows.

This effort continues to grow, but is now in danger of being misunderstood as credit and publicity is being handed over to guitarists.

I do believe that every musician should play whatever technique, instrument, or music he wants, and with no compromises (after all, that's what I've done myself). And I do enjoy a lot of the music by two-handed tapping guitarists, including the novel approach taken by Michael Hedges.

But I also see that misinformation is spreading – about which instrument is in the vanguard of this method, about who created and taught this method to prepare the way, and about which players are taking it the furthest.

Soon, some members of the music press picked up Emmett's case. Josef Woodard asked the question, "Has the inventor of The Stick been overlooked in the Stanley Jordan parade?" Woodard wrote:

"Time has validated Chapman's prescient ingenuity. At the ripe age of twelve years, The Chapman Stick is an established and viable musical tool with an expanding family of players Chapman puts at nearly 2,000. Joe Zawinul, ever the hawk for new music machinery, bought one of Chapman's first five-instrument run, after hearing the inventor playing it in a New York club. The liberating possibilities of The Stick gained public exposure via Alphonso Johnson, Pino Palladino, Kajagoogoo, Peter Gifford of Midnight Oil, Kittyhawk and Bruce Cockburn among other Stick disciples. More importantly, Tony Levin has laid down some of the more signature Stick work in the progressive dominion of King Crimson (his loopy intro to "Elephant Talk" is something of a Stick étude by now). Meanwhile, Chapman himself has recently released the independently produced LP Parallel Galaxy, *showcasing The Stick in folk and jazz-flavored settings.*

"Then suddenly last summer, Chapman's noble cottage industry got a rude awakening. A certain prodigious jazzer named Stanley Jordan was wowing press and public with his pyrotechnical (if musically conservative) two-handed guitar style—remarkably similar to the Chapman tack but minus four strings. In the heat of attention over Jordan's fiery fret dancing, Chapman's pivotal role in the two-handed story was overlooked."

There had been many setbacks along the road Emmett travelled with his Stick, but this was the first one that seemed like it might overwhelm him. Not overwhelm his music or his business. Stick Enterprises was going strong and new instruments and new Stick models were on the horizon. Emmett would make his own music on his Stick regardless – that couldn't be stopped. But overwhelm him in the sense that an injustice was being served and his work, his innovation, and his legacy were the potential victims. Emmett's place in music history would come under fire again in the nineties, but before that, there was much work to be done. Synthesizers had to meet The Stick and an entirely new non-wood Stick model had to be created. Emmett marched on.

Chapter 11 – If You Keep Building It
They Will Keep Coming

From Stick promotional literature during the 1980s:

"It's not often that a new musical instrument becomes accepted as part of the musical mainstream, but The Stick has proven its staying power. The fact that the instrument continues to evolve and pick up more followers is a testimony to Emmett Chapman's original vision."

-Craig Anderton, *Editor-in-Chief,* Electronic Musician

"The Stick is the step into the future. You can take it as far as you want to go – bass, chords, and melody, played live!"

-Tony Levin

"The Chapman Stick is an exquisitely expressive instrument that captivates the attention of the listener. As a player I have enjoyed its full tonal and harmonic range, and have learned much about harmony and counterpoint melody. It is an instrument that brings the creativity of the player to the fore, and gives complete freedom of expression. With the development of the MIDI Stick, the boundaries are limitless."

-Nick Beggs, of Ellis, Beggs & Howard and Kajagoogoo

"The Stick embodies everything I love about musical instruments: the feel of the strings against frets, two-handed polyphony, the growl of funk bass, the cry of rock guitar. And with MIDI, The Stick can now satisfy my lust for technology. For twelve years my Stick has never failed to challenge and inspire me."

-Andy Widders-Ellis, Assistant Editor, Keyboard *magazine*

"It's the most innovative rhythm section instrument I've ever experienced. It has both low and high ranges, access to keyboard sounds via MIDI, and plenty of space for both hands to play on."

-Fergus Marsh, with the Bruce Cockburn Trio

Emmett released two more musical projects during the eighties. First, a video titled *Hands Across the Board*. People everywhere would now have the chance to not only hear his music, but also to see just how he was making all that sound. The visual aspect was crucial for The Stick. Without actually seeing the musician playing, it was too easy to think that simultaneous bass lines, chords and melodies were the result of overdubbing and multi-tracking. He followed up the video with a limited-release cassette titled *Touchboard to Circuit Board*, which was a "demonstration from a live performer's view as to how the synthesizer can be put to use with a fingerboard instrument, in this case with The Stick."

Emmett had long been interested in the possibility of adding the sonic potential of the ever-evolving, electronic sound synthesizers to the expanded, polyphonic potential of fingers on strings offered by The Stick. The first such successful marriage was announced in a May 1981 newsletter from Stick Enterprises. A company called HEAR Inc. had designed a synthesizer that used the vibrating strings of the guitar as the controller for a pitch-to-voltage converter. Once the vibrating string had been translated into a language that electronic sound creating devices could understand, the sky was the limit sonically. HEAR's guitar interface, the Zetaphon, was customized to work with The Stick and Emmett would do the necessary conversions and modifications to The Stick to make it work with the Zetaphon. He embedded a metal sensing pickup into the wood, just ahead of the bridge. He also attached a matching wooden cap containing the electronics onto the rear contoured area, right under the regular pickup housing. A slim 'limo' jack and plug with five hot leads for the five melody strings, fit near the tailpiece. The regular Stick pickups remained fully operational.

"The Zetaphon is a modified guitar synthesizer," wrote Emmett, "customized for The Stick, and is, I believe, the best available, with two channels, additive synthesis, and the full range of controls available on synthesizers. It is polyphonic for the five melody strings, with no crosstalk and with perfect clarity of five individual voices. All the instruments can be imitated, and of course all the sounds in between and beyond."

But it wasn't cheap. The cost to The Stick owner was around $4000 for the modifications to The Stick and the customized Zetaphon with programmer, cords, footswitches and instructions.

With such a light touch and the ability to cover the entire orchestral range, The Stick turned out to be an ideal synthesizer controller. Since the strings are tapped, not plucked or strummed, they vibrate up and down over the pickups rather than back and forth[19] making for uniform and dependable sounds. Because of the prohibitive price tag and because synthesizers were still relatively untravelled terrain for stringed instrument players, the Zetaphon controlling modified Sticks didn't fly off the shelves. As the industry developed new technology, prices came down, quality went up and Emmett would discover interfaces that had a much better reception from Stick players.

---

[19] The vibration of a tapped string travels like a whip down the string, whereas a plucked string vibrates back and forth across a plane.

Meanwhile, the basic Stick itself continued its own evolution, with subtle but often quite significant changes and modifications. Starting in '81, a detachable shoulder strap with a twist-lock stud replaced the fixed shoulder strap. In '82 round-wound bass strings replaced flat-wound strings, giving a brighter, richer bass tone. Also in '82, height-adjustable individual nut screws replaced the rectangular, wooden string spacer and the zero fret. A curved design that swoops down from the neck to the headstock's front surface softened the angular look of the previous ninety-degree angle. "I'm kind of proud of that swoop," says Emmett. "I don't think anyone was doing that then and I can't think of any guitars that have done that since. I did it in a dramatic way. I was always doing what I could to make the instrument look distinctive with sharp, delineated features. Even with the bevelled edges and the curves coming around from the rear bevels, the geometry of the parallelogram pickups and the triangular headstock, I was introducing geometry into what would otherwise have looked pretty much like a two-by-four."

Next, an injection-moulded plastic pickup housing with a metal fibre shielded interior and moulded bobbins for pickup coils replaced the anodized sheet metal pickup module. Fur dampers replaced velvet ones. Black winding heads were introduced as an option and in 1983, an injection-moulded plastic belt hook replaced the sheet metal version. All those were significant improvements. Some changes were aesthetic, some more functional, some, like the new pickup and housing, were significant technological advancements. However, in November 1985, The Stick itself would take a huge jump forward with an entirely new Stick entering the picture.

Up to this point, with the exception of a few experiments with alternative materials like Lucite, Sticks had always been made from wood. Whether ironwood, ebony, purpleheart, or rosewood, the common denominator was always wood. Wood worked great, but it was labour intensive. In 1985, in an effort to free himself from a lot of the hands on production responsibilities and create a Stick that was capable of accepting a good setup from the outset, Emmett introduced a new injection-moulded version of The Stick made from a stiff, black polycarbonate resin, reinforced with tempered spring steel.

The engineered thermoplastic was like a combination of stone and metal. It was injected like molten lava into a specially designed mould, which produced The Stick's entire three-and-a-half foot long by three-and-a-quarter inch wide neck/body. The new polycarbonate Stick was smoother and lighter to the fingers than wood and allowed for greater dynamic control. The upper harmonics and note sustain were more pronounced and the low tones were sharper and more resonant. It was also much more stable than wood and less susceptible to weather and temperature changes.

When Emmett designed the mould for the polycarbonate Sticks, he took the opportunity to introduce some other modifications and refinements. The wooden Sticks had used jumbo guitar-type frets. Guitar frets are hammered into place; therefore, you need to use soft metals that have a certain amount of give, so that one side doesn't pop out when you hammer in the other. The polycarbonate Stick frets were glued and locked, rather than hammered into place, so Emmett didn't need to use a traditional fret design or material. He created an entirely new type of fret, larger than even the jumbo guitar frets. The new frets were made out of stainless steel that was exceptionally smooth to the touch and wouldn't wear down like traditional brass, aluminum or other metals commonly used for frets. A patent was issued in January 1987, in Emmett's name, and these new frets were dubbed Fret-Rods™.

The polycarbonate mould was designed so that the headstock and tailpiece were longer, with a small butt added at the tailpiece for resting The Stick in a standing position and protecting and securing the ball ends of the strings.

(One of the first Polycarbonate Sticks and the injection mould.
Photo by Dan Chapman)

The new Sticks addressed another growing need and concern Emmett had; they were less expensive to produce than the wooden Sticks. It seemed like a win/win: the instruments were stronger, more stable, and less temperamental than wooden Sticks and they were less expensive to produce. Emmett passed the savings on to the customer. The Brazilian Ironwood Stick, still in production, sold for $945. The new polycarbonate model cost $825. The polycarbonate was actually intended to replace the production of wooden instruments. Even though that didn't happen, innovations designed for the polycarbonates, like Fret-Rods and the butt at the tailpiece, showed up on wooden Sticks as well.

"The polycarbonate Stick was an effort to mass produce and to get the work out of my hands," says Emmett. "For two or three years I was making only polycarbonate instruments. It was a big decision, a big move. We were always repairing the older hardwood instruments but the only new production at the time was the polycarbonates. It succeeded in that all the woodworking that used to be done was eliminated. It came back as two moulded parts that got sandwiched together. The problem was that the moulded parts, inevitably for injection-moulded parts of that size, were wavy or warped. They were not straight enough for the very low action setups and even plane of the fret tip's playing surface that I needed for the light touch and fast and expressive action. We'd have to finesse them, put shims in place and do compensatory fret work. I insisted on getting the polycarbonates all to play so that they would optimize the playing technique but I ended up needing to add a process that instead of being an advantage, soon became a disadvantage." The time to do the completion work and setup soon became too much. What was intended to be easier and less time consuming than producing wooden Sticks was actually harder and took longer.

"Finally we just gave up and went back to wood," he says. "That happened in 1989 when I was in Finland at the Pori Jazz Festival. I started thinking about Sticks like paper airplanes, Sticks on guide wires, floating Sticks, inspiring thoughts of having them held together and manipulated by cables on the backside and strings on the front side – a Stick that you could see right through. What I ended up with was a compromise. When I got back home, I created an instrument for the first time with an adjustable truss rod. I made it out of the simplest wood I could find, quarter-sawn white oak. I had ads out for The Oak Stick. Ordinary old oak, just like a park bench. That was the ethic behind it. I wanted to keep the Fret Rods, so I did that. Later, I made the Fret Rods larger and about 4 or 5 years after that, to implement them better, I made the grooves an open 'O' shape, when viewed from the side, rather than the 'U' shape in the polycarbonate. The open 'O' meant that the Rods would slide in from the side and restrict any upward movement.

"To this day, we still set up and repair the polycarbonate instruments," he continues. "On each one I take a trajectory and set my course as to what I'm going to do to get the action down, to make it play like a new instrument. I decide whether or not to put an adjustable truss in so as to create the right profile on the top plane of the fret tips. The main goal is to make it adjustable for the lowest tapping action and lightest touch. If the work is done right and the action is low, the tone is there, the intonation or true octaves are there, the speed is there, the expression is there, and something that people overlook, finger dynamics are there. You can just lay a string down on the fret to get the quietest note and then you can really hammer down with the full velocity of your finger tip to get a loud note, so it approaches the true dynamic range from piano to forte."

Around the same time as the polycarbonate Sticks made their appearance, a new way for The Stick to act as a synthesizer controller using MIDI (Musical Instrument Digital Interface) entered the picture. This new technology was much more user friendly, had a lower price tag and was greeted much more enthusiastically by adventurous Stick players than the Zetaphon. Emmett showcased the new technology on the *Touchboard to Circuit Board* cassette.

This interface, which enabled The Stick to act as a synthesizer controller, was built by Canadian company IVL and was based on their guitar-to-MIDI technology (essentially, it was their Pitchrider 7000 model, with software modifications to accommodate specific Stick characteristics). Only the five melody strings were MIDI interfaced. The bass strings were too low in pitch to track with speed and accuracy.

The *Touchboard to Circuit Board* liner notes, written by Emmett, read:

> *In my hybrid approach to fingerboard synthesis, I play The Stick in the foreground with an 'orchestra' of synthesized sounds, colors and textures behind me. But the orchestra is in my pocket (so to speak). I control it live in a variety of ways – selected sustained notes over which I play clean Stick lines, rhythmically echoed lines, unison melody and chords with the instrument, and transposed parallel lines.*

> *I make no attempt to play the synthesizer as a lead voice, although I could do so. I keep the melody and bass strings of The Stick in the foreground. With these modest goals, a guitar type MIDI interface such as IVL's can work surprisingly well, especially with the right internal software and sensitivity settings.*

With this successful MIDI interface, The Stick, which already covered the guitar and bass range, could now sound like any instrument one could dream up and infinitely more previously unimagined. IVL's stringed instrument MIDI technology and the necessary modifications to The Stick added $900 to the cost of The Stick. For about the price of a second Stick you could have a universe of sounds at your fingertips.

A new instrument requires a new name, and Emmett decided on The Grid™ for this and all future Stick synthesizer controllers. The name took the original concept that The Stick was a blank musical slate to the next level. The Grid was a sonic and tonal blank slate waiting for the creative artist to take it wherever they may go.

Canadian musician Fergus Marsh was one of the first professional players to embrace The Grid. Marsh played Stick on some of Bruce Cockburn's most commercially successful recordings, including two of his biggest hits: "Lovers in a Dangerous Time" and "If I Had a Rocket Launcher." Cockburn has always pushed his own musical envelope, repeatedly reinventing his music and continually surrounding himself with new musicians.

Dennis Pendrith was the bass player in Cockburn's band before Marsh. Being an adventurous player himself, Dennis had heard about The Stick and on a trip to New York, had seen one in a Sam Ash store and bought it. He played it on a couple of Bruce's songs in the late seventies and early eighties and used it live in concert.

When Bruce was putting together the band that would record *Stealing Fire*, arguably his most popular album, he wanted something new and immediately thought of The Stick. Fergus's brother, Hugh Marsh, was playing violin with Bruce at the time. When he heard Bruce asking around if anyone knew of a good Stick player, without hesitating, Hugh offered the services of his brother Fergus. What Bruce didn't know was that while Fergus did have a Stick, he hadn't had it for very long and hadn't been able to spend very much time figuring out the instrument. "I was still trying to figure out where all the notes were when I got the call from Bruce," says Fergus.

When Bruce phoned Fergus and invited him down to a rehearsal, Fergus needed very little convincing. He brought both his bass and Stick and kept reaching for the bass, which he was much more comfortable playing. Cockburn kept saying, "No, I want to hear that Stick." It was trial by fire for Marsh.

Stealing Fire was released in 1984. Fergus would record four more albums with Bruce, culminating in *Bruce Cockburn Live* in

1990. The Live album featured some of Bruce's biggest hits performed in trio: Bruce on guitar and vocals, Fergus playing Chapman Stick, MIDI Stick (Grid) and singing background vocals and Michael Sloski on drums. Emmett saw the trio perform in Los Angeles and said it was one of his proudest moments. "Bruce was there playing guitar, there was a drummer and everything else – bass, keyboard, horn lines – all the other guitar parts were coming out of Fergus. It was amazing." Emmett's vision for a self-sufficient universe of sounds had been reflected back to him through another artist.

(Fergus Marsh live with Bruce Cockburn.)

Two Grid models emerged: one, a hybrid model with all the regular Stick strings and the regular Stick electric pickup plus a MIDI pickup under just the five melody strings, the other a full ten-string Grid. The ten-string Grid looked like The Stick but had no electric Stick pickup, only the MIDI pickup. The ten strings were grouped into melody and bass sides, but the strings of each side were of the same thin gauge (.010 in the melody and .012 in the bass) and tuned to the same high pitch. The full Grid was a total synthesizer controller, with no possibility of natural Stick sounds. Any tuning could be programmed into the accompanying computer software: traditional Stick tuning, all manner of Stick tunings with fourths and inverted fifths in all registers, pitches transposed individually or in groups, guitar tunings, double bass tunings, even a single sequence of all ten strings. The tuning was wide open and could be changed simply by tapping a footswitch. The complete 10-string synthesizer system cost $1,450 for the double rack space IVL Pitchrider box with pickup and preamp installed plus the cost of The Stick.

On *Touchboard to Circuit Board* Emmett played a black polycarbonate Stick with the IVL MIDI pickup under the five melody strings. The MIDI pickup ran a Yamaha TX7 keyboardless synthesizer, controlled by a Commodore 64 computer. He had his regular pedal board with fuzz, a Patch of Shades and a phaser for the bass side. All the songs were original compositions.

Information about Touchboard to Circuit Board
By Emmett Chapman
SIDE 1

Where Parallel Strings Meet – *The synthesized voice chosen for this improv has an attack like a glockenspiel and a sustain like synthesized strings. The Stick melody triggers the synthesizer when I press on the Shades pad. I select certain notes to sustain. They accumulate to become a huge chordal voicing of strings, over which I play clean Stick lines. There are some unison Stick-to-synthesizer solos, and some 'big band' chordal passages where*

186

the synthesizer is transposed down a fifth, giving me four notes for every double-note interval that I play.

The Stick melody is sometimes straight, sometimes filtered, with fuzz sometimes added. My left hand plays a driving rhythm on the five bass strings. Although they go by fast, all of the bass notes are clean, and they define the harmonic changes in rhythmic patterns. It is as if a drummer had tuned a couple hundred trap sets to all of the possible chords and their inversions, and could then instantly jump from one set to another and play any pattern he chose through the chord changes.

Fingers Interwoven – The voices go from 'Chop Bass' to 'Glass Harmonica' to 'Koto.' The Stick melody crossfades from the natural sound to a wah with synthesizer. I play some bass string harmonics. The technique used here is that of two hands interwoven in a 'fingerpicking' style, the right thumb working with the left fingers on the bass strings, and the left pinky working with the right fingers on the melody strings. It's a reciprocal arrangement, like having six digits on each hand!

Firing On All Twelve – The synthesizer voices include a raspy brass sound in the trombone register, and an exotic double-reed kind of sound. The Latin bass-percussion is an exploration of polyrhythms based on twelve – three fours, four threes, and two sixes. The Stick melody is fuzzed. The synthesizer is in unison with Stick melody, with some stacked sustain notes, over which I play fuzzed Stick lines.

Blues For One – 'Timpani' and 'steel drums' voices are triggered in unison with Stick melody, or else transposed down a minor third and up a fifth. My right hand plays single and double note melody over a walking bass in the left. Mid-song, the rhythm

187

changes to a Latin feel. The double note passages, made up of major and minor thirds and sixths become full-fledged four-note chordal voicings with the transposed synthesizer.

SIDE 2

Four Shifting Elements – Again I use the ten-fingered interwoven technique as in the second song, but with synthesizer echoed to reinforce the rhythm by creating an independent, arpeggiated line. The synthesized notes are sounded after The Stick notes are heard, and are repeated several times by a Boss DD-2 digital delay pedal.

The voices, all transposed up one or two octaves, are in the following order: harp, a kind of oboe, vibes, 'Chop Bass,' a wooden flute, glockenspiel with an exotic synthesized sustain, a brass sound, vibes again, brass again, marimba, and the vibes.

With this 'fingerpicking' technique I have in my hands four elements of an orchestra of sounds, any one of which can be the focus, while juggling the remaining three. One element is the bass in the left hand. One is arpeggiated chords in the right hand. One is the right thumb selecting higher notes on the bass strings. And one is the left pinky selecting lead notes on the high melody strings. Yet another element is created by the echoed synthesizer, which is brought in and out by Shades.

From this interwoven texture I wander into the more conventional Stick technique of left-hand bass and chords accompanying right-hand melody.

Triple Play – The voice of the synthesizer is brass in octaves. The wah on the instrument melody is cranked up to 'high Q,' and the fuzz is switched on. With my right foot I press the sustain foot switch, and with my left foot I shift my weight onto the Shades pad to select the notes to be sustained. Then my right hand plays a fuzzed Stick melody on top of it all. My left hand plays a loose version of the Latin bass-chord percussion, punctuated occasionally with louder fills from the right hand.

Touchboard to Circuit Board wasn't as widely released as Parallel Galaxy. It served more as a demo and snapshot of Emmett's musical directions at the time, a direction that included exploring the sonic possibilities that technology could add to his two-handed tapping technique. The analog, real world, physical method met the digital, electronic, otherworldly sound of musical synthesizers. Once again, Emmett didn't draw boundaries and say that The Stick could only sound a certain way or be played in a certain style. All was fair game, and again he went exploring.

The *Hands Across the Board* video completed Emmett's triple play of personal musical output during the eighties. Thirty-five minutes long, *Hands* showcased The Stick and Emmett – seven songs, originals and standards, all performed solo: "Brazil," "Backyard," "Somewhere," "Parallel Galaxy," "Spain," "All the Things You Are" and an improvisation. The improvisation was taken from Emmett's performance at *The Soundboard Guitar Concert.* The video starts with the Soundboard improvisation. Emmett looks confident and sounds strong as the curtain rises. He stands centre stage with his Stick, already in action, tapping, searching for a theme to explore. Although he looked calm and composed, in truth, Emmett was rattled and thrown off his game. His name was announced, he stepped on a footswitch to activate a specific sound, he tapped his Stick and the wrong sound came out. As he tapped a little more, both on The Stick and on the footswitches at his feet, he couldn't find the sound he had wanted to start with. He quickly realized that he had no choice but to go with it and see what he could do. The resulting improvisation sounds stunning, good enough to lead off the entire video. A mistake, accepted and embraced led to places never imagined.

The rest of the video shows Emmett performing in studio with a new black polycarbonate Stick. The five melody strings are MIDI interfaced to his TX7 – an orchestra of sounds from one instrument and one man. Interspersed between the performances, Emmett talks about his music and The Stick. Much like he did at the live clinics, he goes into detail about his two-handed tapping, the origins of his technique, his moment of discovery and the journey of innovations that led to The Stick. All of this delivered in his confident, knowing, soft-spoken yet self-assured way. It's all there for everyone to see and hear.

Emmett released all of his music through his own label: Back Yard Records. True to form, Back Yard Records was entirely handled by Emmett, Yuta and Stick Enterprises. The Chapmans bypassed the hoops and hurdles of the entertainment business and kept matters in-house. The control Emmett retained over his own music, his publishing and his artistic freedom outweighed the benefits of the marketing infrastructure and financial backing of a large music company

Electronics weren't the only way players searched for different sounds from The Stick. At players' specific requests, Emmett built several custom instruments. Allan Holdsworth ordered a short-scale Tenor Stick, tuned in a 'double guitar' tuning. For Canadian Allan Marcellus, Emmett built a fourteen-string Stick, seven bass and seven melody, with the bass and melody strings on opposite sides – an 'uncrossed hands' tuning. Sticks with fretless bass sides were an option. The guys in Kittyhawk convinced Emmett to make a longer

Stick – 38 inches rather than the standard 34 inches. The long Sticks had two lower frets and extra frets all the way up to the pickup housing, which extended the range in both directions. Holdsworth wanted less. Kittyhawk and Marcellus wanted more.

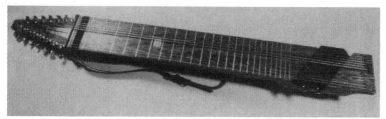

(Allan Marcellus's fourteen string Stick.)

As always, custom tunings were welcome, Emmett never being one to stand in the way of a musician's inspiration. Sticks with double-guitar tunings, guitar and violin, guitar and standard bass in fourths, bass in fourth plus bass in fifths, single sequences of strings, left-handed (reversed) models and other Sticks in more exotic configurations all came out of Emmett's shop during the eighties. Emmett even used some of these tunings himself. Specifically a double-bass tuning he used on an album project with Japanese composer Ryuichi Sakamoto.

(Short-scale tenor Stick, like the one Allan Holdsworth ordered.)

(Emmett with a custom-made Stick for Kittyhawk. Photo by Dan Chapman)

The Stick even took on a mythical face. In Frank Herbert's fictional world *Dune*, Imperial Troubadours often play "a nine-stringed musical instrument, descended from the zithra, tuned to the Chusuk scale and played by strumming." Herbert's fictional instrument, a baliset, sounds "much like our well-known guitar" according to Herbert's description.

For his 1984 film adaptation of Herbert's novel *Dune*, David Lynch needed a baliset. He wanted something like a guitar or a lute but different, something that looked at the same time ancient and futuristic. He found The Stick, but through its music first and not the instrument itself. Mado Most, a friend of Dan and Fred Cory from the Vanilla Rain days, was working for Dino De Laurentiis, *Dune's* production company. "She arranged for me to send them an audio cassette of "Back Yard," which I did," says Emmett. "I recorded a simple audio cassette on my home recorder."

Lynch liked what he heard first and then later what he saw. "I spoke to several people," Emmett continues, "and then finally to David Lynch himself. I went to his office. He made a drawing, which I took home with me, of how he envisioned the baliset based on The Stick. Then I got involved with the business people to draft a contract together. It was basically for the sale of two Sticks, one for conversion into the baliset and the other for them to have in the studio for whoever wanted to play it. I visited him twice more at his office and talked with him a couple more times on the phone. The rest was business with the production company."

Throughout the movie, Lynch explores alternate forms of energy production and generation. The Stick as baliset reflects that search. A spinning wheel and sounding horn were attached to the tailpiece to power and amplify the instrument. Ornamentations that looked like sparkplugs were added to the headstock, implying that the baliset was able to generate its own electrical power. The fictional instrument created the energy needed to amplify its sound simply by the action of tapping the string. Actor Patrick Stewart played Gurney Halleck, *Dune's* noted baliset player, in the film. The instrument makes only a brief appearance in the director's cut of the movie, as Stewart plays a short recital for the fictional nobility. The music in the soundtrack, while Stewart mimes his baliset playing, is actually the original audio cassette of "Back Yard" that Emmett sent to Lynch.

(Dune Stick or 'Baliset' body.)

"Later on," says Emmett, "Kyle MacLachlan, who played the lead role in the film, called us. He had ended up with the second instrument and wanted to take Stick lessons. I said, 'Yes it would be great. You'd be very welcome to come over,' but he didn't follow through."

The Stick fit well with the musical aesthetics of the eighties. New wave musicians were creating new sounds and looking for new musical directions. New shapes and designs were welcome in fashion, music and pop culture. For guitar players, speed was in. Eddie Van Halen, Yngwie Malmsteen, and a host of shred-rockers, who measured their worth by the number of notes they could cram into a song, led the way. Two-handed tapping put breakneck speed at guitarists' fingertips. Some of those guitarists tried Sticks. Van Halen phoned Emmett one day and said that he had to have two Sticks right away so that he could perform in duo with his brother Alex. Eddie arrived at Stick Enterprises one afternoon with a six-pack of Mickey's Big Mouth beer. Emmett set him up with an instrument and sat back, letting Van Halen experiment. "I just watched him play," says Emmett. "It was amazing to watch his creative process at work. He would start with simple little parts and they would evolve nonstop into complex pieces." Eddie was supposed to return the next day and place an order, but he never showed up. Emmett later heard that he had gotten in a minor car accident on the way to Stick Enterprises, but that was never confirmed.

Emmett influenced much of this new two-handed tapping guitar crowd. One can often trace the path of two-handed shred guitarists back to Emmett with far fewer than six degrees of separation. For example, highly sought-after studio and session guitarist Jennifer Batten, who herself has inspired countless guitarists to explore two-handed tapping, tells of seeing another famous two-handed tapping guitarist, Steve Lynch, while both were students at the Guitar Institute of Technology in Hollywood. Lynch had seen Emmett give a clinic in 1979 and was inspired to explore tapping on his guitar. Batten says in a *Guitar Player* interview, "It sounded great to me. I had to follow him (Lynch) at the graduation performance, which was a drag because he whipped out all this stuff that just fried people's minds." Batten would later buy a Stick of her own, but ultimately stuck with two-handed tapping on guitar.

Jazz players were interested too. In a *Los Angeles Times* interview published November 30, 1986, guitarist Joe Pass is quoted: "I'm going to look into the 'Stick,' the instrument Emmett Chapman invented, on which he uses that same note-tapping idea. Oscar Peterson has one; as a pianist, using both hands to produce notes and chords, he can use the same principle."

While Joe Pass and Eddie Van Halen may have been interested in The Stick, they didn't take that leap forward and actually make the instrument a regular part of their musical arsenals. By the late eighties this trend was playing itself out. Big name musicians would be interested and excited about Emmett's tapping and The Stick, but after an initial burst of excitement, they often wouldn't take the instrument anywhere. Development and exploration fell to Emmett and more increasingly, to an emerging host of young, amateur, unknown or lesser-known musicians. With the exception of Tony Levin, Fergus Marsh, Alphonso Johnson, Nick Beggs and a small handful of others, The Stick was absent from the major concert stages. However, musicians seeking to set themselves apart from the crowd were increasingly embracing it at the grassroots level. A real Stick community was emerging. Where Emmett was once alone, he now found himself joined by other musicians from all around the globe who were sharing tips, techniques and music with each other.

Blake Lewin created a resource of lessons, reviews and Stick related articles, bound them together, and sent them out via mail order subscription under the title, *Sticking Together*. In issue #6, July – September 1989 he writes:

> Sticking Together *is a network of Stick® players interested in sharing ideas and experiences about The Stick with fellow musicians.*
>
> Sticking Together *is not a magazine, it is a* network *[Lewin's emphasis]. It is a chance for Stick players to share their ideas and feelings about The Stick over the many miles that separates us.*

Unlike other traditional instruments, there is no bank of information and/or music available to The Stick player from which to draw. It is my feeling that in these early, developmental stages of Stick playing Sticking Together *can expedite the growth of Stick playing by allowing information and knowledge to pass freely among musicians. Growth and knowledge can only be attained through the exchange of information and the expression of ideas.*

To join the network you didn't need to be a professional player. All that one needed was "a sincere interest in The Stick and desire to share ideas, comments or questions with other Stick players." Members were required to "write at least one page of ideas, comments, or questions about The Stick." Exercises, song arrangements, gig reviews and upcoming show notices were all encouraged. Participants would make enough copies for everyone in the network and mail them to Lewin, who would then compile all the submissions and mail them out to each contributor. Along with Lewin, Bob Culbertson, Larry Tuttle, Steve Adelson, Andy Widders-Ellis, Marco Cerletti, Dale Ladouceur, Roli Mack and Troy Sharp also contributed. All these musicians were becoming significant and influential Stick players.

A movement was underway, gathering momentum with every passing month. The idea behind the implementation of Lewin's *Sticking Together* would soon become infinitely easier as the Internet revolutionized the way information was exchanged. As technology changed and more and more people joined the ranks of Stick players, new challenges would present themselves. Demand on the already strained confines of Stick Enterprises increased exponentially. Emmett and Yuta found themselves busier than ever as they sought to meet the needs of a Stick community that was spreading out around the world. On the musical front, as the eighties turned into the nineties, Stick players would begin to reach the same virtuoso level that Emmett had achieved. A whole new level of player emerged, the Stick community grew in leaps and bounds, due largely to the ease with which communication could travel through cyberspace, and Stick Enterprises would face its greatest challenge by far.

Chapter 12 – New Players, Instruments and The Biggest Challenges Yet

"'Stick,' 'The Stick,' 'The Chapman Stick Touchboard,' and 'The Chapman Stick' are all registered trademarks of Stick Enterprises, Inc., and must be used as adjectives to describe 'a new musical instrument,' or 'a stringed instrument,' etc.

"So if The Stick is used in your publicity please refer to it the first time on the page as in these examples: The Stick®, The Chapman Stick® musical instrument, The Chapman Stick Touchboard® stringed instrument, and so on. First letters of the trademark should be capitalized. After this first reference, you can use the words 'The Stick' with first letters capitalized, but without the R-with-a-circle.

"Such usage will prevent these trademarks from becoming general language, and thus belonging to anyone who would want to name their product 'The Stick,' as happened to 'Xerox,' 'escalator,' 'thermos,' 'cellophane,' etc. Thanks!"

-Emmett

From Stick Enterprises Newsletter, December 1981

"If you have a lawless environment like the high seas, you can have a tradition of pirates that profit from it. So now you could make that metaphor with the Internet. It's like the high seas. It's unregulated, as I think it should be (and the ocean is free too) but in the process you get pirates. You get people who are targeting you and marauding others and looking for the booty."

-Emmett to brother Dan in the ChapDoc production of Emmett *2009*

As the eighties turned into the nineties, a definite Stick community had emerged. Very soon it became clear that the greatest potential for the instrument and Emmett's technique lay not in the hands of the Jeff Becks or the Joe Zawinuls. Rather, it lay in the hands of the supporting cast of Tony Levins, Alphonso Johnsons, and more increasingly, the amateur players, all of whom were tapping into new sounds and new music. If the eighties was a time when The Stick was finding a home as a supporting instrument in groups, then the nineties marked the emergence of the solo virtuoso Stick player. Many players had been playing Stick for years, and Emmett was finding company alongside himself at the forefront of the Stick vanguard.

In more or less 20 years, Stick Enterprises had grown from a dream and a personal passion into an established business with customers around the world. By 1989 the Yucca Trail house in Laurel Canyon, which had served as Stick Enterprises' world headquarters since 1974, had become too small to handle the growing business, Stick production and still be a home for Emmett and Yuta. Yuta was also worried about the ever-present risk of neighbourhood canyon fires. One hot, dry summer day, fire did break out in the hills around their Yucca Trail home. Evacuations were ordered. Yuta gathered as many important business documents as she could and put them outside in metal garbage cans so they would be safe should the fire destroy the house. Luckily, the fire spared their home. Unfortunately, Yuta forgot to put the lids on the cans and water bombers had dumped water all over the hills, filling the cans and soaking all the vital documents.

Emmett searched Los Angeles for a new home for the Chapmans and The Stick. He was drawn to the beach and concentrated his search on properties near the ocean. It was Yuta who found a house with room enough for a workspace, in familiar territory at the western end of the San Fernando Valley in Woodland Hills. The house that would become their new home and the new Stick Enterprises was located just two blocks away from the house that Emmett had helped his dad Laverne build some 40 years earlier. He had come home.

In August 1991, Stick Enterprises sent out a newsletter to Stick owners and other interested musicians. The 11-page newsletter began with an update from Emmett on the state of the Stick world:

Stick Wire – *Stick Enterprises Newsletter, August 1991*
<u>*I, Em, the Editor*</u>

This newsletter is being mailed out to Stick players of all countries, with greetings from Yuta and me at Stick Enterprises, and our wholehearted support of your musical activities. It has been very rewarding to witness the wide variety of outstanding music being put forth on The Stick, and this year in particular, is an eventful one in that regard.

With this "Wire" we're proud to furnish you with listings of Stick recordings old and new, and to inform you of Stick events, live performances, alternate tunings, recent write-ups of various players, and new instructional materials and accessories now available. We also wish to announce a CD Stick player collection album now underway.

Enclosed with this newsletter is our brochure describing the new wooden model of The Stick. We also have available other materials, articles and literature, and can send you the following free of charge upon request:

A feature article in a popular newspaper in England, The Independent, *about a very successful "Stick Night" at London's*

Jazz Café with artists Jim Lampi, Marco Cerletti, Trey Gunn and Nick Beggs.

The Grid – magazine articles by Stick players Andy Widders-Ellis of Guitar Player *magazine and Steve Adelson, and also our Grid newsletter of August 1988.*

Excerpts of reviews praising the Stick work of Canadian Fergus Marsh on a recent world tour as part of Bruce Cockburn's trio.

A letter from Tony Levin telling of his studio recording projects.

A published interview with London Stick player Nick Beggs of Ellis, Beggs & Howard.

A letter from Billy Graham Evangelistic Association telling of Nick Beggs' featured Stick work with English rock singer Cliff Richards' trio, which was broadcast last winter by satellite to an estimated one and a half billion Asian viewers as part of Dr. Graham's "Mission World" television ministry in 44 languages. The song, "Thief in the Night," is a Christian rock video production with Richards' vocals, Stick, keyboards and drums, including a solo by Nick.

Emmett wrote of an upcoming compilation of top Stick players:

"Back Yard" Gardening

I'm happy to announce that we are about to reactivate our old record company, Back Yard Records, and will soon be releasing a Stick artists collection album (on CD and cassette) of some of the very best Stick performances ever recorded – one song each by ten or twelve players. Among these featured artists will be Bob Culbertson, Frank Jolliffe, Jim Lampi, Marco

Cerletti, Fergus Marsh, Leo Gosselin, Andy Widders-Ellis, Ron Baggerman, and others, including myself. This album will document an incredibly wide range of sounds and rhythms, and a great diversity of individual Stick techniques and musical directions. Stay "on the Wire" for a more detailed description of this collection album, along with purchasing information, coming soon in our next newsletter.

Qualified Stick teachers were teaching Emmett's technique to players around the world. The newsletter announced the following events:

Seminars & Workshops

A European "Summer Stick Seminar" will take place August 12 through 17 in the Belgian village of Rossignol in the Ardennes Mountains near Sedan, France.

Stick player Daniel Shell of Belgium has organized this event with sponsorship by the Gaumes Jazz Festival and the Jeunesses Musicales of Belgium. Stick players Jim Lampi of London and Frank Jolliffe of New Jersey will be teaching classes along with Daniel.

Chalet lodging and meals will be provided, and there will be visits and sessions with some of the Jazz Festival artists. Also, Frank will do a Stick concert at the Jazz Festival.

Daniel plays the 12-string Grand Stick, but with a unique tuning – mirror image intervals on both groups of strings, the bass group tuned one octave below the melody. He regularly tours Europe with his contemporary classical group "Karo".

We expect approximately twenty Stick students to attend, as indicated by the response to our May 10 announcement mailed out to European Stick players.

Stick classes, concerts and recitals were held at the National Guitar Summer Workshop from July 1 to 5 at Scripps College in the Claremont College complex in Orange County, California. Stick instructor Frank Jolliffe, who has been conducting Stick seminars for NGSW for the past five years was joined by Alphonso Johnson and myself.

The class was divided between Frank and Alphonso, and I taught two days of afternoon master classes. Frank and I also performed in concert for the entire student body. Alphonso conducted a class recital, with each student playing through his sound system and he played his Grid fingerboard synth controller. Stick players came from all over the U.S., as well as from Europe, Canada and New Zealand, in response to our general mailing of the NGSW announcement.

This event proved to be a welcome meeting of players, as well as an intensive musical learning experience, according to the many comments we received afterward.

I did a ten-day tour of Japan last November, playing clubs and outdoor concerts, and conducting music store workshops for very receptive young Japanese musicians. This tour was extremely well organized by our Japanese Stick distributor, ATL, with television and music magazine coverage as well. These events took me to Tokyo, Kyoto, Osaka, Kofu, and Yokohama, my first (and very enjoyable) visit to Japan.

Major label releases featuring Stick players included *Kneeling At the Shrine* by Sunday All Over the World, a quartet featuring Robert Fripp on Guitar, his wife Toyah Willcox on vocals, drummer Paul Beavis and Stick player Trey Gunn. Gunn also played Stick on Wilcox's *Ophelia's Shadow*. Tony Levin was busy, as always, providing Stick work on the Yes alumni's recording *Anderson Bruford Wakeman Howe*, Mike Mainieri's *Steps Ahead*, Ute Lemper's *Games of the Heart*, French singer Jeanne Mas's release *Les Crises de l'Ame*, Laurie Anderson's *Strange Angels*, Richard Thompson's rock recording *Amnesia* and a self-titled release from Tim Finn.

Nick Beggs, who was introduced to the Stick and brought it into play with the pop band Kajagoogoo, was busy with a new group called Ellis, Beggs and Howard. They released an album titled *Big Bubbles, No Troubles* and three singles from that album. The way The Stick made itself a featured part of Ellis, Beggs and Howard echoes a familiar tune. "It (Stick) wasn't my main instrument in Kajagoogoo," says Beggs, "and it wasn't my main instrument, at first, in Ellis, Beggs and Howard.

"We were writing material and I kept getting The Stick out. They said 'put that away, we want you to stay down in the low end.' I finally said, 'Look, if you want me to find a voice, I'm going to have to use this instrument.' Finally I came up with this riff and this progression, which was the middle eight of a single that hadn't been such a big hit for Kajagoogoo. We worked it up into a song and it was a hit for us. The song was "Big Bubbles, No Troubles" and it was a hit in Europe. So from then on they said, 'No, don't pick up the bass guitar, pick up The Chapman Stick.'"

The early nineties saw a new addition to the Stick family. Even though Emmett experimented with different numbers of strings and built the 14-string Stick for Allan Marcellus, he never thought he would add strings to The Stick. "On the contrary," he says, "I felt that there might develop some demand for a simpler version with less strings." But in 1991, Emmett added strings and Stick Enterprises announced the production of The Grand Stick™. According to the press release, The Grand Stick was a "bigger, wider Stick with twelve strings instead of ten, which combined all Stick tunings – standard, Baritone and Double-Bass – into one super fingerboard with yards and yards of improvising space to play upon." The first Grand Sticks were made from oak, which in spite of their larger size, actually made them lighter than the 10-string ironwood Sticks.

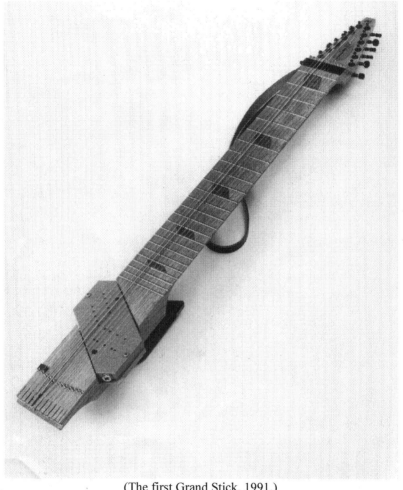

(The first Grand Stick, 1991.)

The key to The Grand Stick was the rear adjustable, surface exposed truss rod that Emmett had first implemented with the oak 10-string Sticks in 1989. A truss rod applies tension at the rear surface of the instrument's neck, in an opposite direction to the natural pull of the strings. This counteracts the pull of the strings away from the frets or fretboard and allows the player to control the distance between the strings and the instrument's neck. Sticks had always had truss rods, but not until Emmett created his patented rear adjustable truss were Stick players able to adjust the tension of the truss rod themselves. This opened up a whole new range of hardwoods that didn't need to be as rock solid as either ironwood or the polycarbonate material Emmett had been using. With a hard-shell case, a stereo cord, a truss rod adjustment wrench and *Free Hands*, Grand Sticks sold for $1593 and were an immediate hit with old and new Stick players alike.[20]

Along with new Stick technology, new computer technology was revolutionizing the way the world communicated. The Stick world grew by leaps and bounds in the nineties, mirroring the growth of the Internet. The Internet is a visual, auditory, immersive and interactive medium. As the Internet grew, Stick images and video could be seen more and more easily, almost instantaneously in fact, around the world. Perhaps most importantly, Stick players could now communicate with each other. The days of musicians learning two-handed parallel string tapping in isolation were over. This new medium served the Stick's performance-based, musically explorative philosophy exceptionally well. Add the fact that Stick players have always tended to be technologically savvy and embracing of new ideas and you have a recipe for success. Blake Lewin's mailing

---

[20] My first Stick was an oak Grand Stick #492, purchased on December 14th, 1993.

system and Emmett's newsletters were quickly giving way to Internet chat groups, promotional Websites, message boards and voluminous email.

After a couple of earlier message boards and discussion groups had started and failed, Vance Gloster established an Internet listserver in 1992 titled *Stickwire.* He based the chat group around his simple philosophy: "This will be a place where like-minded people can gather to share ideas, trade stories, teach and learn together." He set himself up as a moderator, to oversee the list's smooth operation and to tone down any disputes before they got out of hand. People from all over the world could instantly be in touch with one another, sharing their thoughts and opinions with a receptive, like-minded audience.

"The Internet had been around, in one form, or another since the late seventies," says Gloster, "but it was a very small community of people. You could only get on the Internet in the seventies and eighties if you were either a student in a university that was connected, or you worked for a contractor who was doing business with the government or military.

"In the early nineties they were just beginning to take the wraps off it and allowing regular folks to get on the Net. There was this feeling on the Net that this was the end. It had been a club of like-minded people, people who had been technologically savvy. It was a very new thing having all these people who were artists, musicians, and dedicated hobbyists on the Internet instead of just scientists and computer programmers.

"Stick players had always been a little bit disconnected – if you take any one city or town, there aren't very many of them. So it was the perfect community for a Global Village experiment. You have this 'small village' of people who just happen to be scattered around the globe, who are communicating via the Internet.

"Stick was particularly enabled by the Internet. Where print and television media were about a broad casting of messages, the Internet, especially in the early days, was about narrow casting. Small groups of people spread out over large areas could all pursue a single, narrow interest. With something like The Stick you quickly get a small group of people who share the same feelings and in moments, they are in touch with each other. The world shrinks. The Stick world crystallized into a connected global community."

The first Stick discussion groups quickly turned into sites for flame wars, and places where attacks rather than support became the norm. Gloster's goal was to succeed where others had failed and make an Internet group in the model of a 'Victorian Club,' where members policed themselves and everyone acted openly and freely but with respect. It took time and at first, the flaming continued on *Stickwire*, but over time Gloster's vision was realized.

"My role was much bigger earlier on," he says. "Early on, what I really had to do was to evangelize to people and try to create this 'friendly community.' In most other Internet newsgroups and mail lists there is a certain air of contentiousness. What I thought we needed to do was to be a community where everybody liked, or at least respected each other and we had an exchange of views but we didn't flame each other.

"So in the early days I did a lot of evangelizing and cajoling people to make this vision of the list understood. Ultimately I was successful, because these days when someone goes outside of this idea, I don't have to say much of anything. The other people on the list have gotten this idea and they will actually say something to folks.

So I've been able to go back to being more of a Stick player and less of an active list owner who cracks the whip and tells people 'yes you can do this and no you can't do that.' These days, I end up being just another participant on the list most of the time."

Stickwire wasn't just about sharing ideas. Young players found a home and a receptive ear for their music. Players were made and careers started through the connection with supportive and enthusiastic music fans on the list. "Very early in *Stickwire* I had gotten some Stick albums," Vance continues. "I found this record by this kid that I just loved. I loved one tune in particular and I talked on the list at length about how great a CD it was. So he decided to quit his day job and go and be a Stick player fulltime – that was Greg Howard.

"I just loved his song 'Charmed Life.' I felt it was one of the greatest things I had ever heard. I talked about it on Stickwire and Greg has told me that that was something that helped him. Seeing that kind of feedback helped him have the confidence to think that he could actually go out and be a Stick player, to take off his training wheels and jump into it.

"I'm not trying to take credit for what Greg has done. Certainly his great playing is all due to his efforts, not mine. But I think that when musicians can see people recognizing what they are doing, it encourages them to go out and do more with it than they would have done otherwise."

Greg Howard, of Charlottesville, Virginia, was about to become a major player in the Stick world. The story of how he came to The Stick is worth noting. He came to The Stick from a keyboard background, not guitar or bass, and it resonated so profoundly with him that not only would he go on to become one of the key virtuoso Stick players, but he has also become a leader in the Stick community and a key part of Stick Enterprises.

"I had dabbled with keyboards without much formal training for years as a kid," he wrote in response to the question: How did The Stick change your life? "I was moved to get into improvisation by seeing Oscar Peterson when I was 15. I studied sax and clarinet, then I got into synths.

"I had been a fan of King Crimson since the pre-Tony Levin days, and saw them in 1981 and 1984, only realizing the second time what was musically happening with Tony playing The Stick!

"At 20 (early 1985), while looking for a new synth, I happened to ask about a Stick at Chuck Levin's Washington Music Center. In those days synths were still either very lame or very expensive. They had a used Stick and I plugged it in and started messing around. What got me wasn't the two hands equal two parts capability. It was the sound and the expression I could achieve right away on the instrument.

"The Stick rivalled the keys and sax for my attention for several years, and I played each with a certain mediocre degree of competence. Each type of instrument represented a portion of the sonic spectrum to me, as I was mainly into improvised performance and recording.

"Then in 1992, after not really knowing how to play for 7 years, I started to work on my first CD. This recording would be composed songs, all solo, and without edits or overdubs, in a jazz style, with melodies and solos. Each track had to be a complete performance, because all I had to record with was a DAT machine. I set my keys and sax aside and dug in, just The Stick and me. Five hundred hours, hundreds of takes, and many mistakes later I had *Stick Figures*[21]. I also had a new ability to really play The Stick that I would never have developed had I continued to rely on my electronics and mediocre sax and keyboard skills to say what I wanted to say."

Stick Enterprises was sailing along. Emmett, Yuta, daughter Grace, and one additional part-time employee, kept Sticks rolling out and finding eager hands to tap them. Emmett was becoming more and more tied up with the business side of the operations and was playing and performing less, but with Don Schiff, Bob Culbertson, Steve Adelson, Larry Tuttle, Greg Howard, Tony Levin, Nick Beggs and others joining the ranks of top players every day, Stick music was in good hands. But just when the ship seems to be sailing the straightest and all seems calm, the biggest storms often strike.

Ironically, Emmett, The Stick and Stick Enterprises would face their biggest challenge because of their biggest successes. The Stick may have been the first instrument designed to explore Emmett's unique two-handed style of tapping, but it isn't the only instrument that has since been designed to play this technique and it won't be the last. In the early nineties, The Stick was by far the most successful two-handed tapping instrument and had the highest public profile and the largest customer base.

Beginning in 1993, Emmett and Yuta began to become aware of some occurrences that caused them alarm. Among other things, confidential names and addresses of Stick owners were given, without Stick Enterprises' knowledge or permission, to competitors. These competitors then sent Stick owners unsolicited mailings that were often disparaging to The Stick professionally and Emmett and Yuta

---

[21] This is the album Vance Gloster promoted on *Stickwire*.

personally. Classified ads appeared in music magazines advertising new Sticks by companies falsely claiming that they represented Stick Enterprises. The source code of a business competitor's Website was filled with hundreds of repetitions of Stick Enterprises' trademarks, "Chapman Stick" and "Stick," along with prominent Stick players' names, which weighted Internet search engines to provide the competitor's name when the keyword "Stick" was searched. A business was advertising itself as "A Chapman Stick Consignment Shop" without consent from Stick Enterprises. Someone allegedly posing as a utility company did a TRW credit check and obtained information about the Chapman's finances, mortgages, credit cards, creditors, loan institutions and social security numbers. Information obtained from this report was combatively reported on *Stickwire*.

Anyone familiar with Jay Conrad Levinson's book *Guerrilla Marketing* will recognize the tactics: align yourself with a successful product, present yourself as an expert in the field and use any and all means to promote your product in unconventional ways. In other words, capitalize on someone else's success. If you're a small business, all the better – attach yourself to a successful big business and use their success to create your own. One of the problems with this was that Stick Enterprises wasn't a large company. "The reason it may look so large," Emmett wrote in his defense, "is that I've been building these instruments in my shop in steady, uninterrupted production runs for the past 23 years."

Emmett continued, "There are about 5000 Stick instruments out in the world, an unusually large percentage of which are played by excellent musicians in public places. Thus it appears larger than it is, also making us a large target for opportunists. But, in fact, my wife Yuta and I run the entire business, as we have since 1974, in our house, with our daughter Grace heading the shop production, and one part-time worker – that's it."

In 1997 Emmett and Stick Enterprises filed a lawsuit in an effort to stop what he considered to be misuse of his trademarks, and online attacks against Yuta and him personally and Stick Enterprises professionally. "It was about use of my trademark and their business tactics. It wasn't about any other instrument," says Emmett. "It was not about intellectual property like patents or designs but about use of our trademarks to identify, associate and sell, and in the process, criticize us and our work professionally and personally. They created a misconception," he continues, "distorted the story and said that I couldn't tolerate anyone competing with The Stick, although there had been several earlier competitors that we had had no problem with[22].

"They claimed that I sued them for copying The Stick," he continues, "which simply wasn't true. They were scaring our customers and alienating them. Then our established customers would call Yuta and they'd be nervous, they'd be secretive and they'd be fearful. Yuta would have to try to sail through that and operate professionally on a daily basis. It was miserable for us in the mid-nineties, well before the lawsuit was going on.

"We had no choice but to file a lawsuit," Emmett wrote in 1998. "The other side knows that my work is arduous with production, repairs, custom orders, R&D and running a business. They know that I'm not only preoccupied with the intricacies of production and administration, but also with maintaining my musical growth as a Stick player and teacher. And so they manipulated a campaign of words, trademarks, listings, slogans and published disparaging

---

[22] For example, The Hamatar, Robert's Roto-Neck™, the Bunker Guitar, Stuart Box's Box Guitar and a few others.

214

comments in printed and electronic publications. They have worked at all levels to identify themselves with our product and trade names, with the customer base of trained and excellent Stick musicians, and with the public goodwill we have cultivated since 1974.

"For three years we tried to contend with the rumours, hate and alienation that the defendants personally fostered among our customers, unlike anything we'd experienced in 23 years of being in business. Yuta and I have had to respond to persistent and sometimes extreme attacks on a daily basis by telephone, e-mail and correspondence, and have had to maintain a professional bearing while defending our reputation, products, services, and our business actions."

Emmett goes on to state that he has "voluminous written and electronic evidence of this persistent derogation, ridicule and insults, always by the same detractors." The voluminous evidence consisted primarily of e-mail correspondence sent directly to Emmett and Yuta, Stick Enterprises and others, along with postings on *Stickwire* and a host of other Internet chat groups.

"We cannot conduct our business, lead our lives, and continue creative improvements while [others] are actively manipulating our customer base, Stick history and the Stick community, all the while identifying themselves with our trademarks in headlines, interviews, lead paragraphs of interviews and articles, and in their classified ads," added Emmett. Perhaps what hurt most was that a small group of long-time Stick players and supporters, who were once considered friends and colleagues of Emmett and Yuta, turned their backs on the Chapmans and publically contributed to the attacks on Emmett's reputation. "Our business is so personal," says Emmett. "It has to do with my musical aspirations, the craft of making the instruments and customer service. It's just our whole life and so these attacks hit particularly hard."

The lawsuit went to court and on March 12, 1998, the Honorable James L. Wright gave his findings and settled the case. In his findings Wright stated, "The allegations of unfair trade practices must fail for lack of competent evidence." He called into question Emmett's claims of confidentiality agreements and determined that negative remarks made in public against The Stick were in the realm of opinion, and therefore not libellous or slanderous. As to Emmett's "voluminous written and electronic evidence of this persistent derogation, ridicule and defamation, always by the same detractors," the court stated: "I cannot and did not consider the Internet communications. They are absolute hearsay… How do you authenticate Internet communication? The only way I know is to request admissions or depositions by the parties where they admit that they posted things. Given that, there is no evidence before this court of anything that would constitute impairment with, an economic impairment, or special damage to Mr. Chapman. I don't have a single dollar amount anywhere of any special loss."

The Internet communications were not authenticated and therefore were inadmissible in court. Without them, Emmett's claims against his detractors lost their power. Emmett also couldn't prove a *specific* dollar amount for loss of sales, although it's hard to argue that business wouldn't have suffered due to the overwhelming amount of time and energy needed to mount their legal action. The case was settled and the terms of the settlement were ordered confidential.

"If other manufacturers were to sell their instruments and credit me with the specific method that their instrument is designed for, I'd be happy enough," says Emmett. "I don't mind the musical instruments. They tried to make it look like I did, that they were competitors and I couldn't tolerate it. That was part of their story."

Despite the attacks, the larger group of Stick players, friends and fellow musicians rallied around Emmett. "Even during the most painful times there was so much good support coming in. It was rewarding and that provided much of the incentive to continue," Emmett says. "There was so much momentum we had and that kept me going. I was defending myself not just legally with a lawsuit, but on a weekly, almost a daily basis on our forums, because the pressure would really build. There was so much misinformation that simply had to be refuted. So I got the reputation, for a while, for some pretty strict posts. After the lawsuit was over, I considered it settled. We were the ones that initiated the settlement. But they didn't settle in spirit and kept fighting and arguing and disparaging us online. We didn't fight back for years after that. There has been a lot of really negative ammunition online against us. They stirred up flames on our forums and then crowed about it on theirs. They did it for years."

These days, the lawsuit years seem like a thing of the past. Even though, according to the parts of the settlement terms that were made public, all of the online confrontational materials were supposed to have been removed and it was agreed upon by all parties that Stick Enterprises' lawsuit was not frivolous or malicious, you can still find remnants online. For the most part though, it seems like people have moved on. When the occasional flame appears on an Internet forum, it seems to be quickly extinguished. Emmett does continue to defend his trademarks, as any trademark owner is legally required to do (if one doesn't defend their trademarks then one runs the risk of losing them). But for the most part, it seems like people have gone back to focusing on making music and pushing the boundaries of instrument design and manufacturing.

The lawsuit and online attacks weren't the only challenges that Emmett and Yuta faced during the 1990s. While the business and personal attacks may have turned Stick Enterprises upside down, two more events shook the Chapmans, both metaphorically and literally, and tested both their strength and resolve.

On March 29th, 1991, Emmett's mother Venetia passed away. She had been struggling for years with multi-infarct dementia, a series of small strokes that become more and more debilitating over time. Laverne nursed Venetia through her illness. While still dealing with Venetia's passing, on August 4th, 1991, the car Laverne was driving in was rear-ended and careened into a parked truck. He broke several bones, was hospitalized and never fully recovered consciousness. He passed away three months later on November 5th. As the oldest of the four children, Emmett found himself not only grieving for the loss of both his parents but also handling all the personal and legal family obligations associated with his parents' passing.

And as if that wasn't enough, just as the personal attacks which led to the lawsuit were heating up, on January 17th, 1994 at 4:31 a.m., the earth literally moved. The Northridge earthquake, a devastating seismic event officially measuring 6.7 on the Richter scale (unofficially measuring as high as 7.1) struck. Although the quake only lasted about ten seconds, the damage was immense. Over 80,000 buildings were damaged or destroyed, 57 people were killed and over 9000 injured, seven freeway bridges collapsed and 212 others were damaged. The estimated dollar cost of the disaster ranges from $20 billion to $25 billion. The shaking was felt as far away as San Diego and Las Vegas. Stick Enterprises, Yuta and Emmett's home, was about seven miles from the epicentre.

Fortuitously, on January 1st, 1994, Yuta and Emmett did a tour of their house and work areas with a video camera for insurance purposes. "We were advised to do that and it seemed like a good idea," says Emmett. "Then the earthquake hit and everything in the house was broken and strewn around. Everything ended up in the middle of every room. Furniture was broken, all the nails had been pounded out of the drywall, the front part of the house had collapsed a couple of inches. And so after the earthquake, we took that video camera around again and recorded all the damage.

"We didn't have any electricity, water or gas for several weeks. We were using the water out of our swimming pool, a convenient reservoir of water. I bought a little Honda generator, which I still have, and could run two things at a time, like a TV and a coffee maker or a light and a toaster. That was it. That's how we got by."

In another stroke of good fortune, before the earthquake struck, the house directly across the street from Stick Enterprises was being remodelled. The Chapmans needed a home. Yuta contacted the owner and inquired about renting the house while theirs was being rebuilt. "They said to give them a couple of months to finish construction," says Emmett. "But we said we really couldn't wait, so we moved in while they were still building." Emmett, Yuta and Stick Enterprises had a temporary home and both business and family life continued.

"It was a year and a half, close to two years from the time of the earthquake to when we moved back into the house," says Emmett. "We moved back in 1996. The soil had to be re-compacted and a huge 20-foot wide V-shaped gully was dug across the front of our house and the house was put on stilts. Just the earthwork alone took two-thirds of the re-construction time. They created a seismically engineered foundation and concrete slab, with extra rebar reinforcements and metal fittings in the house so that it would rock nicely in future earthquakes."

In spite of the legal battles, family loss and natural disaster, even though he was pushed to his limits physically, emotionally and financially, Emmett and Stick Enterprises carried on. The lawsuit and the time Emmett spent gathering information and formulating his case took valuable time away from running the business and playing his music. "Emmett did a really good job of keeping everything on an even keel," says Greg Howard. Greg was an integral part of Emmett's support system, both during and after the lawsuit. In 1998, shortly after the suit was settled, Greg moved to LA and helped Stick Enterprises return to normal business operations. "It affected Yuta and Emmett mostly in terms of what they were doing on a day-to-day basis," Greg continues. "That was probably the biggest stress for them. He really made an effort to keep the business end of things going, in spite of everything else that was going on. I remember people criticizing him at the time for putting all this time into defending himself. Not his friends, but the other side would say that he should be making instruments instead of focusing on this lawsuit. And of course, he would have liked nothing better. It's an ironic situation, but he had to do what he could to keep things going."

The rest of the Stick world marched on as well. Bob Culbertson released a set of three instructional videos. The videos progressed from the very basics of Emmett's technique through to advanced compositional and sub-techniques. These marked the first in-depth video breakdown of the technique.

Greg Howard added a written educational Stick resource. His *Stick Book™ Volume 1* joined Emmett's *Free Hands* as one of the key written references for Stick instruction. Greg and Emmett worked together to create a new notation system for *The Stick Book*. This system, which they dubbed "Staff Tab"™, "superimposes string/fret position and fingering information onto a three-dimensional realm of standard music notation (pitch, rhythm, expression)," writes Howard in the book's introductory pages. He goes on to explain: "Conveniently, standard piano music uses two staves of five lines each to represent the positions of the notes played. Each staff serves as a grid upon which we can overlay the Stick's strings – the five melody strings are represented on the treble staff, and the five bass strings on the bass staff. The exact fingering for each note is indicated as well. In order to accomplish this, we have added three new graphic devices to standard notation to present the necessary six dimensions of Touchboard® playing, while still including the traditional pitch, rhythm and expression information of standard notation."

Chapman's and Howard's system replaced traditional music notation's round note heads with differently shaped note heads representing the four fingers as in Emmett's *Free Hands* method book.

Numbers above the staff and a highlight on the specific staff line corresponding to a Stick string, indicated on which string and which fret the note would be found. New music, new instrument, new notation – it all fit together.

Two new Sticks joined the family. Before Emmett released The Grand Stick he had always thought that he would have to make simpler Sticks with fewer strings, rather than bigger ones with more.

In May, 1996 that's just what he did. To appeal more to bassists who weren't so interested in the treble register, Emmett began experimenting with Sticks that still had all the features of a standard instrument – low action, light touch, angled more vertically for both hands to approach from opposite sides – but that focused on the bass end of the sound spectrum. The first Stick Bass™ (SB7) was thinner than the standard 10-string Stick and had seven strings. The lowest pitched string was tuned to a low B and was on the outside of the instrument, as on a regular bass guitar, rather than running up the fretboard's interior like on a regular Stick. The rest of the strings were tuned in one group of ascending fourths, rising in pitch from that lowest outside string.

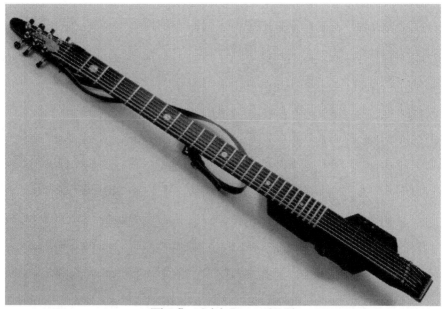

(The first Stick Bass – SB7.)

Emmett created the SB7 in the temporary Stick Enterprises facility, across the street from the earthquake damaged Stick Enterprises. "We set up the temporary workshop in the garage, like in our other home, but it was quite a bit narrower," says Emmett. "I always associate that narrow Stick with that narrow garage." Two dozen 7-string Stick Basses were made before Emmett decided on eight strings for The Stick Bass, with the same basic dimensions as the standard 10-string Stick and a slightly wider string spacing.

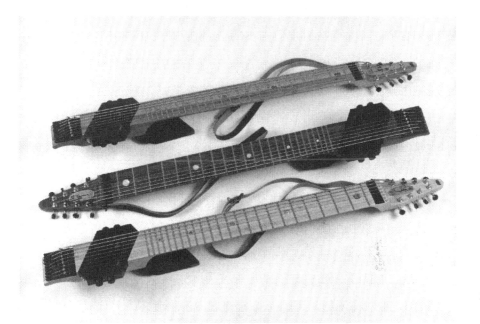

(Three SB 8s.)

The eight-string Stick Bass (SB8) was tuned in ascending fourth intervals, but all other features were the same as the standard 10-string Stick. Bassists could now concentrate on two-handed bass lines without worrying about the two sidedness of The Stick. Traditional bass techniques would also lend themselves to The Stick Bass. "Since the strings are spaced farther apart," writes Emmett in the press release, "this instrument also adapts well to conventional picking and plucking bass techniques. By placing your plucking hand close to the bridge, you can 'dig in' more, as on bass guitar, even though the strings are set up for the very low, light touch, two-handed tapping action." At that time, an SB8 cost $1,395 plus $195 for the hard-shell flight case.

The next step was to build an instrument that accommodated all common bass and guitar techniques and worked equally well for tapping, strumming, plucking, popping or any other electric stringed instrument technique. To create that instrument, Emmett collaborated with another revolutionary, boundary pushing instrument designer, Ned Steinberger. Steinberger had already made a name for himself, first by designing an award winning bass guitar for Stuart Spector, and then designing his own radically different Steinberger basses and guitars.

Ned began his career not as an instrument builder, but as a furniture designer. He brought his innate, intuitive understanding and appreciation of ergonomics, form and function to guitar and bass design. The most striking feature of the Steinberger bass was its minimalism. The instrument had a small body and no headstock. Much like Emmett did to the guitar when he first created The Stick, Ned stripped the bass guitar down to its essential components and created an extremely playable, user-friendly instrument. Emmett and Ned set out to build a universal fretboard, an instrument that incorporated seamless transitions between two-handed tapping and conventional bass guitar techniques.

"I met Emmett through Tony Levin," says Steinberger. "Tony had played Steinberger basses in the past and also Stick, of course. Emmett called me. I think he saw that the market for tapping instruments wasn't fully encompassed by The Stick and that some kind of crossover instrument would be interesting. He felt that it might be constructive for us to work together on it, which is what we did."

The finished product, The NS Stick™, incorporated much of both Steinberger's and Emmett's characteristic designs. Eight strings, tuned in fourths, with the lowest bass string on the outside like The Stick Bass, extremely low action and a flat, uniform fretboard came from the Stick side. A headstock-less design, small body, tapered bolt on neck and string spacing that widened as the strings reached the bridge came from Steinberger's designs. The body shape was important and Ned and Emmett went round and round trying to decide on the right design. They both wanted to keep the theme from the Steinberger basses and guitars of the '80s, which they did, but they reversed the contours. In some ways, the look of the NS Stick resembled the old Freedom Guitar, with its small body, long neck and minimalist design. Some features were unique to the new instrument, like a jointly patented damper (Chapman and Steinberger, Sept. 17th 2002) that could be engaged or disengaged. This allowed the NS Stick strings to either ring out and be plucked or strummed as open strings, or to be muted, which dampened unintended notes when the tapping finger came off the string. Ned also designed unique bridge and nut side-saddles that were adjustable with a hex-wrench and offered infinite increments of height gradation. The bridge design and nut side-saddles were new and allowed for unprecedented control over individual string height. Over time, the NS Stick became more Stick-like, with rear-bevelled edges on the neck and Fret Rails[23] rather than more traditional guitar frets.

"I brought, probably more than anything else, a fresh outlook to how you might make the instrument" says Steinberger. "Emmett's original idea was a more bass oriented Stick instrument. My approach

---

[23] Fret Rails are diamond shaped frets mounted and anchored into place beneath the fretboard surface with the 90-degree peak rising above the fretboard. Rails were an option to the Fret Rods as of 2000 and have now replaced the Rods on all Stick models.

was a more guitar *and* bass player oriented Stick. So the NS Stick is designed to be tapped or plucked, with the string spacing to accommodate that. All of this was worked out together, of course. In the end, the standard tuning is a very standard eight-string ascending fourths. I think it makes it more viable for a lot of players just to pick it up and play.

(The NS Stick.)

"It was a good project for me because I like to figure things out. I'm not really a stylist primarily. I'm interested in how things work and how to make things work. For example, once you go from a headstock to a headless instrument, and you make that big of a change, all of a sudden you have a whole new set of detailed problems to deal with. Solving those problems effectively is a big challenge that I enjoy and a big part of my job."

On a lighter note, a near disaster with the NS Stick was narrowly averted just as the prototype instrument's final form was taking shape. Emmett, Greg Howard and Steve Adelson had been performing at a trade show and were taking Steve to the airport to catch a flight back to New York. "We had *the only* NS Stick prototype, the very first one with us," says Greg. They had some time and decided to stop at a *Denny's* on the way to the airport to get something to eat. "We didn't want to leave the NS Stick in the car so we brought it into the restaurant," he continues. "We ate, got up, got into the car, started driving to the airport and suddenly realized that we had forgotten the instrument! We whipped around, rushed back and thankfully it was still there, sitting right where we had left it."

Stick Enterprises, Emmett and the Stick community survived the turbulent nineties. Although beaten and battered they were far from broken. There were casualties along the way, but for every player who abandoned ship it seemed like there were several new musicians who discovered both the instrument and Emmett's technique and committed themselves to exploring two-handed music making. As the century changed, The Stick continued evolving. Even though the troubles of the past had not been entirely resolved and the group of people trying to build themselves up by tearing Emmett down continued, Stick players (or Stickists as they would soon become known) continued to refine their techniques, discover new approaches to the instrument and make outstanding music. Emmett charged full on into the 21st century, much like the picture brother Dan took in 1974, with Stick firmly in hand and taking on the world with all his passion, focus and desire.

Chapter 13 – Welcome to the New World

"...The engine section of the band consists of the batterist and the holders of the 'grand sword.' The batterists are essentially collectors of short sounds for rhythmic use, and most of them have a closely guarded personal library consisting of thousands of these...

"...Working closely with the batterist are the holders of the grand sword. Our closest relative to this is the bass-stick. The grand-sword players – there are normally three in a band – usually dictate the modal environment and pace of the song by their opening parts. The other musicians quickly adopt a position relative to this... The relationship between the sword players is complex and hierarchical, but the idea seems to be that they should end up sounding like one impossibly competent player, interlocking with each other in a completely indistinguishable manner. Normally this is achieved by the players operating in different registers – what we might call baritone, bass and ultra-bass..."

– *From Brian Eno's* A Year with Swollen Appendices: Brian Eno's Diary, *Faber and Faber, 1996.*

The imaginary musical world described above came from a game Brian Eno designed to encourage improvisation while working on David Bowie's *Outside* recording. Reeves Gabrels, Erdal Kizilcay, Mike Garson, Sterling Campbell, David Bowie and Eno were to imagine a musical culture and invent roles for the musicians within it. The musical landscape they created is reminiscent of Frank Herbert's

Dunescape or maybe the bar scene from *Star Wars*, both ancient and futuristic at the same time. Once again, The Stick fit.

The question remains though: where will The Stick end up in the real world? The instrument was conceived through Emmett's two-handed tapping on the Freedom Guitar. In the seventies it was like a child taking its first steps in a big wide world. The eighties found The Stick offering adventurous, innovative musicians new ways of accessing and creating music. Stick virtuosi joined Emmett throughout the nineties. Both the instrument and the players emerged from these formative years with momentum on their side.

Now, well into the 21st century, the Free Hands technique is pushing 50 years old. The Stick is in its 40s. But, both are still infants in the life of a musical instrument. Emmett is still the final stop in the production line for every instrument. The Stick family now includes seven different models made from various hardwoods, bamboo, graphite and a new instrument detailed later in this book. There are three different pickup modules, four if you include a modified MIDI pickup. Each Stick model is fully adjustable in every way that a stringed and fretted musical instrument can be adjusted. Almost any tuning and setup option can be realized. Each Stick can now be as individual as each player. A new production model is close to completion[24]. Emmett has just received patents for a new design that should take him out of the manufacturing line, if all goes according to plan. Musically, Emmett has talked of playing with a percussionist and maybe a wind player – just clean Stick, no effects, the sound of fingers tapping strings against frets.

The Stick community stretches around the globe. Active communities of players have cropped up in Australia and Japan,

---

[24] This new model, The Railboard™ is now in production. Read more in Appendix II.

throughout Europe, South and Central America and across North America. Gatherings of players are a common occurrence. Events are regularly held in Michigan, Virginia, France, Spain, Germany, Western Canada, Southern California and elsewhere. Always, the events center around a player who takes it upon him or herself to organize and promote the events. Glenn Poorman, Jim Meyer, Derek Dallenger, Toshiaki Kanamaru, Karsten Roeth, Olivier Vuille, Guillermo Cides, Greg Howard, Steve Adelson, Qua Veda, Tom Griesgraber, Casey Arrillaga, Virginia Splendore, Irene Orleansky and I, to name only a few, have hosted events. Each features instruction from noted players who have become equally notable teachers of Emmett's technique. Public performances at these events feature both students and teachers and bring both instrument and music to new eyes and ears. Online, www.stick.com is the home of Stick Enterprises. Vance Gloster's *Stickwire* remains a vital and vibrant forum for the global community. In 2002, Manny Tau launched www.stickist.com giving a new voice and a new face to the online Stick community. Since then, stickist.com has grown into an essential resource for players and fans of The Stick and Stick music and reinforced the moniker 'Stickist.' Most recently, Gene Perry created the Free Hands Academy.

As of this writing, Gene's Academy has hosted two major Stick events as well as an ongoing series of online chat sessions where Stickists from around the world gather for weekly chats about all things Stick.

New Stick players are making names for themselves and familiar names, many of whom have had Sticks in their hands for decades, continue to push the boundaries. Stickists Tony Levin and Michael Bernier joined forces with King Crimson drummer Pat Mastelotto forming a trio called Stick Men. They took their show on the road, touring through North America and Europe after releasing their debut recording, *Soup*[25]. The list of exceptional players is long and getting longer. Both Stick Enterprises and Manny's sites have extensive connections to excellent players who are performing and recording all over the world.

(Free Hands Academy, August 2014. Emmett is in the front row, far left. Photo by Dave Cohen of BHE Photography, courtesy of Gene Perry.)

It seems like the bad blood from the lawsuit years may truly be drifting into the past. In 2007, the Website most critical of Emmett and his claims to his technique was taken down. Other instrument manufacturers are creating instruments designed for Emmett's two-handed parallel string tapping technique, but fewer and fewer people are looking to sources other than Emmett for the origins of his technique.

But with all that good news, the world still waits for the Stick's Jimi Hendrix, Eddie Van Halen or Jaco Pastorius to light the mass

---

[25] In 2010 Markus Reuter replaced Bernier. The group has released four more recordings to date.

culture on fire and push The Stick to the same heights as its electric guitar and bass counterparts. On the big stages, The Stick remains out of the center spotlight and continues playing its supporting role. In the small clubs, on the fringes, in circles where boundary-pushing musicians live, it's a completely different story. The Stick has found a home.

Emmett's friend since his teenage years in the San Fernando Valley, Bill Kettman, is now an architect. When we talked about his memories growing up with Emmett, the talk led to the art of building buildings and a connection to any act of creation soon arose. "Creation is a dream or an imagining about something existing that may never exist, but does exist in your mind and in your heart," he said. "It comes from your experience and it comes from stretching what you know is possible to include the improbable. In that process it's OK to say that there is some reason why it's impossible. You work around the impossible by imagining that the problem has been solved. If that is true, what do you do then? What follows? In the dream, somehow the new way of imagining away from a problem creates the solution that was never there before."

I see enormous similarities in what Kettman says and what Emmett has done. The solution to Emmett's problem existed before he created the means to realize it. He knew how to play and what he wanted to play, the instrument grew from there. The impossible became possible and real because in his hands and his heart he already knew the solution; the mind just hadn't realized it yet.

As I look back on how all this came together I'm still left searching for the one grand idea, the statement that encapsulates what Emmett has done. It's tough to pin down. Even now when I talk with Emmett about his work and The Stick, the ideas flow and feed off each other and I have to struggle to get them going where I'm trying to take them. At some point in the conversation I usually just give in and let the thoughts and the ideas go where they want to go. The beauty is in the unmapped journey. Like the man on stage, alone with his instrument, looking for new musical horizons, we talk and the ideas flow, intertwine, blossom, dead end, breathe, take on their own life.

When we talk, Emmett is always jovial, always searching. Sometimes contradicting, quick to call me to task, steadfast in his beliefs. Serious but far from solemn. For a man who has always followed his own path, my attempts to pin him down to any one route often seem futile. One thought leads into another, the questions take us in unintended directions, but still I move ahead, hoping that at some point the picture will become clear.

Three moments sum up Emmett for me. The first was during that first visit to Stick Enterprises, after we had played tennis. I had brought my Stick (Oak #492, a 7+5 Grand). Emmett asked me if I'd like him to have a look at it and check the setup. Of course I did. Not only was I excited to have Emmett do some work on my instrument, but I also thought, 'here's my chance to pick up a few tips from the master.' Emmett put my Stick up on his worktable, turned on the lights above (angled so that the light bounced off and he could check the individual string heights) and then effectively disappeared. I leaned over to look closer and asked some questions, but his attention was completely focused on The Stick in front of him. It wasn't like I was being ignored. It was more like he was so absorbed by the fine tuning he was doing to my Stick, that the rest of the world around him ceased to exist. My questions seemed to pull him out of another world. I quickly stopped interrupting and just watched. I've never seen that quality of focus and attention again. He was utterly and completely in the moment.

I'll also never forget the look of joy, pride and admiration in Emmett's eyes during a concert of Stick players at a NAMM[26] Show Stick Night. The show was at *Molly Malone's*, a small Los Angeles club. With each player that took the stage, Emmett watched with rapt attention. There was the sense that he was amazed and in wonder with what all the diverse musicians were able to do with their Sticks. When Emmett's turn to play came, he took the stage as their equal, not the 'Father' of all and in truth the reason why all those players were there in the first place. When I played that night, I improvised over top of recordings of various musicians I'd interviewed talking about their experiences with The Stick. As I came off stage, he rushed up, grabbed my hand and said how overwhelming and wonderful it was to see his work reflected back at him in that way. Humility and gratitude.

The final piece of the Emmett puzzle fell into place while I was working at Stick Enterprises in 2004. For about six months I helped out with the business side of things, helping Yuta, answering phones, dealing with orders, and filling in wherever I could. The workdays started mid-morning. One morning I arrived a little early and rather than swing past the *Starbucks* to kill some time with a coffee, I went into work to catch up on some emails. As I made my way upstairs, I could hear Emmett playing in his studio beside my work area. It was magical. No stage, no audience (save me), just a masterful musician playing with joy, freedom and abandon for no one but himself. I quickly figured out that if I arrived 30 or 45 minutes, even an hour

---

[26] National Association of Music Merchandisers annual trade show. This one was the winter show in Anaheim, California.

early (although that was pushing it a little) more often than not, I'd be treated to a live soundtrack of Stick music. What a way to start a day. Regardless of the invention, regardless of the production and design, regardless of the esoteric world, social, political and philosophical views, for me, Emmett is first and foremost a musician – the rarest of musicians who can connect with his own personal muse and bring unique and enriching music into the world.

With those three experiences as my guideposts and with the rest of this book as the background, I did (what I thought was) my final interview with Emmett for this project.

JR: As you look back on your life, your work, what makes you the most proud?

EC: I'm generally proud of my life. That kind of wraps it all up, a life's work. I just can't let any one single thing stand out, neither the music nor the manufacturing and the repairs nor the public relations and customer service, nor any of it. It's all wrapped up into one thing. My life includes Yuta, our daughters, also an extended family of Stick players and performers and I try in my own inimitable way to be the proud father of it all. Yuta, my life-long partner, is then by inference, the mother of it all.

JR: Can you name a couple of defining moments in your life?

EC: (Long pause) I'm normally not all that responsive to moments. The thing that has guided me all my life, since childhood, is philosophy – a philosophical mind. It's a guide to right actions and a guide to sane relationships with other people. Philosophy is important to me the way religion is to other people, but I kind of rejected my religion and found a different path.

JR: Ok, then define that philosophy in a few words.

EC: It's very broad. It includes everything I could possibly include in the universe. There would be some contradictions in there too and I could enjoy those contradictions, just like a work of art has contradictions. Sometimes designs clash. Sometimes they're harmonious. You'd want all of those things. It's a philosophy that includes psychology, which I first came to in junior high. It includes cosmology that I got later, reading esoteric books and Scientific American. *It includes how I'd like the world to be if I were king, economics, politics, technology. It's just very broad. It's everything.*

JR: OK, the obvious question then, is how would you like the world to be if you were king?

EC: (Laughs)

JR: You couldn't just toss that one up there without expecting me to take a swing at it.

EC: Well, it would depend on the issue being discussed. I'd have opinions on a lot of issues that were guided by my philosophy. Like, why human nature isn't brought into particular political issues? Why not consider the way things work in nature, human nature and Nature nature, Mother Nature? There are powerful lessons to learn there. I'd have to have a specific question to say specifically what I'd change about the world. When I say king, it's kind of a joke because it implies a benign dictator, a benign king. That's the joke. Certain utopian political philosophers think that's the ultimate. Without that you can't have any system that works really well. So really, I joke about it. I am a believer in democracy and democratic philosophy, how it originated in England and France and spread over here. How we were at a formative time in our nation and implemented those ideals and how we continue to implement them.

236

JR: In the dictionary entry beside 'Emmett Chapman' what do you want it to read?

EC: Just to reflect accurately what my life has been about, which is The Stick – both manufacturing it and playing music on it, teaching others to play music on it and my own musical ambitions with my two-handed tapping technique. The other thing I'm proud about is that philosophy. I've got essays about all that on my musings page[27], but far and away, I'm most proud of The Stick, manufacturing it, inventing it, designing it and playing it.

JR: If you could be remembered for just one thing, what would that one thing be?

EC: Probably a song or a performance, but up there, high on the list, would be my Offset Modal System[28]. Of course, The Stick as a stringed instrument and its playing method are what I work hardest on and strive to nurture most - old Sticks and new, earlier players and latecomers.

JR: Where did you make your mistakes?

EC: One can't be one hundred percent proud because there are always regrets and wrong turns. And I admit to them, not being one of those who proclaim, 'It's all for the good,' or, 'Everything's a learning experience.' Some episodes are just miserable and best to avoid if you can. As for my actual mistakes, I'm not proud of them so I keep them to myself. They're just not 'me.'

JR: Let me rephrase the question: If you had to do it all over again, what would you do differently or would you do anything differently at all?

---

[27] See www.emmettchapman.net.
[28] See appendix I.

EC: That's a question like, 'What would you do if you had a time machine and could bend time?' You'd probably distort time in the process. In this case, if I could have those kinds of wishes, which no one can have, I would probably distort my own life and that old adage would apply: be careful what you wish for. I have regrets in my life when it seemed like I was wasting time, spinning wheels. I did the best I could, prioritized and behaved kindly.

JR: There's always been that pull between being the musician and the creator of the instrument. Dan really hones in on that in his documentary[29]. I remember one of the first questions I ever asked you was "When did you decide to be an instrument maker more so than a player?" I remember the phone line went dead quiet and after a few moments you said, "Well, never." It was a great realization for me that you never stopped being a player and it's always been the music that's driven the creation and development of the instrument.

EC: Yes, it's strange. Both are always at play. I think that I probably look more normal and regular than I really am. I think I'm quite unusual on the inside and I seem to have an ability to tolerate stress forever. I look kind of easygoing so people misjudge me constantly. I'm kind of misunderstood on that score. It's hard for me to even assess myself. I think that hardly anyone would be able to drag out continually leading a double life this long, where you're trying to make one side work to help the other and yet they're so antagonistic towards each other.

JR: But the two sides and the conflict between them, musician vs. builder, allow each other to exist. They're symbiotic. They may be at odds with each other, but they couldn't exist in isolation.

---

[29] Dan's documentary film, *Emmett,* in production at time of this publication.

EC: Well, you wonder about that, maybe with this particular instrument. Stick is not like a Fender guitar, it's not like a saxophone, which was an offshoot from the clarinet. It's an instrument that takes a dedicated player to make it live and put the magic into it. On the production side, you have to strain the limits of technology and materials, the geometric limits of what's possible and implement it into actual production. I used to think of it as an invention of shape, of geometry. In a sense it is. You have mainstream inventions and these days they're often electronic. There's a snowball effect that comes from a mainstream technology that spins off more and more combinations of what's possible in the form of other inventions. I've always said about mine that it could have been invented at any time in the past or in the future. It's independent of mainstream technology. It's truly an invention of shape.

JR: I'm having trouble with the comment that it could have been invented at any time, past or future. I don't know if I agree with that. The string tapping could have been done, and was done before. But I don't think that the technology existed for your 'invention of shape' until you did it.

EC: Yes, electricity of course. Let me rationalize how I express that idea. If I'd really wanted to do this but I'd been living in the 1400s, I would have made an acoustical instrument that you could barely hear. Everyone would have had to huddle around it in a small room.

JR: Or attached it to a large gourd or something like that.

EC: No. Size doesn't help when you're just tapping. In fact, a smaller-sized resonating chamber is really the ticket to an acoustic version of The Stick. When you have big bodies you have to put a lot of energy into the string to make it vibrate, either with a bow or by plucking really hard like on an upright acoustic bass.

JR: So, is it fair to say that The Stick is the musical and physical manifestation of those different philosophies that have guided and shaped your life?

EC: That's true. I try to be guided by an entire faculty of mind and it's a strong impulse. It always has been like that, since childhood. It was like I was creating a code, my own code of conduct. I kind of rejected mainstream cultural codes of conduct. I don't think that's the way to go, but that's what I did, and watching them disintegrate in later generations, I'm kind of glad I did do it independently. That's a big statement isn't it?

JR: It is a big statement but it seems to me that that is what enabled your life and your path to be successful.

EC: It does have to do with my life. People look at their lives when they get older, sometimes even when they're young, and see it either in various states of becoming, or in shambles, a shell of your life if you're on drugs or mess it up or injure yourself badly. There are all kinds of things that can go wrong. I value my life. I look upon it with pride and recognize that it's fragile and it could all be a lost investment. I invest in my mind the same way. I'm diligent about it.

JR: What did you add to the musical landscape?

EC: I blended my creation-from-the-heart with the aspirations of other musicians, and almost got drowned out in the process. The rewards for such sacrifice may seem distant and less personal but are immense.

JR: Let's talk about other Stick players and other musicians for a bit. What are some of your favourite songs from other Stick players?

EC: Songs are just vehicles, carriers for the artist's musical style. They necessarily restrict the style, bringing the player back from the universal and home to the audience. So it's never the song but rather how it's played, who's playing it, and what musical personality is shining through.

JR: All right, how about 10 Stick moments or players that sum up the potential and the sound of the instrument?

EC: Ok, I do that at the risk of leaving out people who I really admire and honour. When I try to answer questions like that, it's always the players that are happening in the moment that come to mind. Currently, Tony Levin playing four movements of Stravinsky's "Firebird Suite" on the Soup *CD. His Stick Men group with Michael Bernier and Pat Mastelotto is very impressive. What Mauricio Sotelo does with Cabezas de cera from Mexico is as outrageous as Weather Report in their prime. It's Stick with electronic drums and a horn player, just amazing. Then there are the people that are on the new DVD[30]. All are incredible players and stylists. Bob Culbertson is on there. Bob and I are probably the biggest purists of playing just straight Stick. He is such a virtuoso. I have nothing but pride when I hear him play. I love his music and his technique and his orchestration just with his fingers. Greg Howard is in there as an excellent teacher, a composer of memorable songs and has an amazing flexibility with The Stick. He plays it according to The Stick. That's something that he probably never appreciates when I say it, but to me, it means a lot to 'play the instrument according to the instrument,' rather than make it sound like a guitar plus a bass or make it sound like something else. They said about electric guitar at the very beginning, when Charlie Christian was playing, that he could*

[30] *Stick Night Live*, Chapdoc, 2011.

play lead parts like a horn right there in his band. People marvelled at that idea – there was a guitar sounding like a horn. But I like the idea of making the instrument be the instrument when you're playing it. I try and do that myself. That's one reason why I have this impulse to have each hand play on all 10 strings and not relegate one hand to one set of strings and one to the other.

JR: Right, which is really arbitrary. When I listen to your early music especially, I hear that the line between the two sides of The Stick doesn't really exist.

EC: That's right. The first prototypes weren't even in stereo for one thing.

JR: And the tuning on the Freedom Guitar that led to the Stick was designed for extended range chords, not a split instrument. I hardly ever play my Stick in stereo. I'm in mono almost all the time, especially when I'm playing solo.

EC: I like to play in stereo, but I also like my Bose PAS system. It forces me to play mono. When you're playing in a club, you don't even want to play in stereo. Playing mono is great because you wouldn't want one part of the room to hear something different than another part of the room.

JR: Back to your Stick moments. You've given me five. I need five more.

EC: Well there are a lot more! I like Larry Tuttle's classical pop approach with Novi Novog. It's amazing that someone would first want to go in that direction with The Stick and then play it so well. On the new DVD they perform a Prokofiev piece. A lot of people know the song and they're going to be blown away. It's sinister, sounds a little like Wagner. It's called "A Love for Three Oranges." I like unusual directions like that. I'm leaving out so many people. I can't even begin to scratch the surface. The resource of players with their own unique styles, talents and dedications to The Stick is overwhelming to me. I can't even begin to assess it or compare them except to more or less talk about what's happening now, like the new DVD, Cabezas de cera and Tony's new release. What Jim Lampi did with Michael Manring on the recording North, *is exceptional. It's coherent front to back and yet within that universe they created is a myriad of sounds and moods.*

JR: I find it really interesting that it's the current players and music that comes to your mind when we talk about great Stick moments. It's not Tony Levin's part on "Elephant Talk", it's Tony's "Firebird Suite." Even though both are revolutionary Stick moments. "Elephant Talk" must have introduced more people to The Stick.

EC: Yes, it was big. Too big for me to understand. I just sort of took it for granted.

JR: Do you remember the first Stick players that turned your head and really knocked your socks off?

EC: Yes! Bob (Culbertson) and Don (Schiff). Do you know why?

JR: No.

EC: They were both playing left hand motors, real funky things. It got to me.

JR: Had you been doing that before?

EC: Yes, but it was like a kick in the butt for me and it became a challenge to develop it further after hearing them do it.

JR: Let's talk about the big name, famous musicians that dabbled with Stick. We've talked in the past about why they didn't necessarily take Stick as far as they initially seemed that they would, why they didn't latch onto exploring the potential of the two-handed technique on the instrument. I'm thinking of Allan Holdsworth and his Stick, Jennifer Batten, Jeff Beck, Eddie Van Halen, those players.

EC: Right, all those guys. I'm not sure if Jennifer actually bought a Stick, but she came to the house and she was interested. Stanley Jordan was too. I have letters from him inquiring about The Stick and promising that he was going to get one.

JR: I came across a newspaper article where Joe Pass said that he was going to explore The Stick.

EC: I remember that.

JR: It was an old LA Times. Joe said that it was seeing Oscar Peterson play Stick that inspired him.

EC: Oscar had two Sticks! I went to his apartment while he was living in LA and gave him a few lessons. Learning to play The Stick was a project of his. He was having hip problems at the time. I think he had just had surgery, so he was having trouble both standing up and sitting down when he played. It was difficult, but he earnestly wanted to learn to play. I remember thinking to myself, 'Here's my idol – and not just *my* idol!' Oscar was one of the most disciplined, creative, superb players I've ever seen. One of the very top, in a handful of the finest pianists and here he had an ambition to play The Stick. I still can't believe that.

JR: There have been so many close calls with really famous players.

EC: Joe Pass lived right in the next canyon to ours. I'd look out my window on Yucca Trail and he was over on Wonderland Canyon, right across on the other side of the mountain I was looking at. That's how I knew him. He reminded me of Tal Farlow the way he continued an idea or a melody line through a lot of chord changes without *having the chords interrupt the melody. That was a sign of being really on top of it as a jazz musician.*

JR: There've been so many opportunities that looked like they were going to take shape and then they didn't.

EC: Well, you don't know which one to pursue and probably didn't give enough importance to one or the other, in hindsight. You don't know when you're spinning your wheels and when you're not.

JR: Why?

EC: 'Why' is the question. Why do some actors make those formative decisions that break them to the public and afterward everything they touch turns to gold? I spun some wheels, and with regrets, but tried to be purposeful and to prioritize my activities. On the other hand, one has to enjoy life and take advantage of opportunities as they come.

JR: Why do you think someone like a Joe Pass or maybe better yet, a Jeff Beck or an Eddie Van Halen would start towards The Stick but not continue?

EC: For popular artists, often the answer is simply time versus money. It's really like invested time versus time to invest. It's more about that. Money can be written out of the equation as invested labour, stored labour, stored time. A person who is already invested isn't always as willing, or more importantly, as able to invest in something new or something that might even be perceived as interfering with what they already do. The instrument has come through people who were not known, who had the time. I'm trying to paint it with a broad brush, but what I'm really saying is a cliché.

Eddie Van Halen's experiment with The Stick was part of a project that he and his brother were working on, to be a rhythm section backing some other artist. In any event, he never used it as far as I know, except for a couple of intense practice sessions at our Yucca Trail house, and so his name doesn't really connect in any meaningful way, except to mention that he had an interest at a certain point in his career, as did Jack Bruce, Jeff Beck, Jennifer Batten, Oscar Peterson, Gil Evans and Joe Pass (who you brought up). There were other famous rock musicians interested in the early eighties.

There's a lot of pressure to keep playing your hits, especially if you listen to your agent and your accountant. But I would say that the artist has to have the capacity to at least know better and not listen to his or her advisors. But I would say the same thing about all careers, regardless of profession. They should listen to themselves and not get influenced by those people who are grooming them. That would be one of the things in my world if I were king (laughs).

JR: So let's make the distinction between Jeff Beck and Eddie Van Halen and Tony Levin and Nick Beggs. All are equally skilled musicians in their own right, but maybe Tony and Nick are far enough away from the center of the stage and playing enough of a supportive role to give them more freedom to dive into playing the instrument?

EC: Maybe that's it. Maybe the bass player's frame of reference is automatically in a supportive role. When he gets The Stick he can be content to be supportive but it also opens up avenues: more strings, more range into the melody side. Tony didn't play a lot of the melody in King Crimson, but he did play some. It was more pattern oriented. Some of the patterns that sound like Fripp's were Tony's.

JR: I know. I remember being blown away the first time I saw the band and realized that.

EC: Tony is probably the exception to a lot of musicians' biographies. Whatever he touches is done with good taste, with forethought. He's an exceptional person. It's my good fortune that he took up The Stick. Greg has tried to frame what Tony brought to The Stick that is different from anybody else. It has to do with the fifths bass tuning and using both hands on the fifths bass tuning. The fifths tuning really opens up bass in a very nice way.

JR: I think I've heard Tony say similar things.

EC: I don't think he ever defined it like that. What I remember him saying is that he'll pick up The Stick for a certain song for tonal reasons, for the attack. He says it's "fast way down low." Those are his words. Fast means that the sound doesn't bloom. It's right there as soon as you hit it. The 'blooming bass' is the upright bass when you pluck it.

JR: I remember you saying once that The Stick is very easy to play, but then it gets hard, very quickly. So I think the instrument itself draws in the kind of people who want to look deeper and go deeper.

EC: That's true. As a commercial product, there would be a disappointment factor for some customers who buy a Stick thinking they're going to get this new sound that they've been hearing since the mid-seventies. When I started, everybody was looking for the new sound and it was synthesizers. I was trying to say, "No, this is an instrument that you play differently. It doesn't sound so different."

JR: There's still a big question looming. Where is all this going? Once you're no longer around what happens?

EC: (Long pause) Well, I really don't think much about the future. I can only just plan in steps ahead that are real to me and interesting. So I guess I'm not really interested in future times. I kind of distrust people who think far into the future and I don't want to be one of them.

JR: I'm not letting you off the hook.

EC: I can tell you more immediate things, like Grace will have a good part of the production. Greg, if he's still able and willing, will be involved in the marketing and our customer/artist relations. Yuta will always be involved. She carries the lion's share of everything that has to do with running our business, corporate and financial things. I don't think The Stick would just disappear. I've got this new model that I'm still developing, which will mechanize a lot of the work that I do and possibly make it so that I don't have to be a part of the production anymore[31]. That's something I'm working on with that end in mind, mechanizing the final part of the production.

JR: That's always been a part of the struggle for you hasn't it, to work yourself out of the equation?

EC: That's right. Isn't that strange?

JR: It is strange.

EC: Some people feel the need to be needed, but I feel the opposite. I don't have huge goals, but I would like to get this new model into production if it's possible. That is, if nothing goes wrong in the last prototypes, if it plays well and holds up well. I've made two prototypes and I've got two new patents pending on the design. The other thing is to do a real artistic production of my own playing and record it on video. I want to put it together so that I'm not just caught in the act onstage, but I'm actually putting out a musical work specifically for its own purpose.

JR: If you could only choose one, which would be the more satisfying accomplishment: creating the music or creating the new instrument?

EC: Well, it would be a close call, but it would probably be the music. Having my music out, published and recognized is the greatest

---

[31] The Railboard™, see Appendix II.

void for me. The Stick is already recognized. The results are in. The music is great. We don't just produce new instruments either. We repair the old ones and make them play like new. Coming up with a new model would be great, but it's not as compelling as actually getting my current music out there.

JR: That's revealing too, like the 'building over playing' and you never chose one over the other.

EC: That's true. I never did. I just held it in suspension. With me it has been a mix of doing any and all things to make The Stick and the playing method work, while at the same time promoting my own music. Before The Stick it was guitar, before that it was singing and all the way back to when I was in grade school. I was performing then but it was with art and drawing and posters.

JR: All different manifestations of the same creative impulse?

EC: In that respect it wasn't even guided by philosophy. It was just an impulse to create things that were polished and finished. A lot of people will spend their lives wanting to be creative but never polish it. They just put up with their mistakes and think that one day they'll be able to perform. But you'll never get there unless you put yourself in that jungle and live there. I already felt that when I was a kid.

JR: You talk about getting back to playing and it almost seems like it's coming full circle. One of my favourite recordings of yours is still the old, scratchy recording of you and Les DeMerle tearing it up at The Cellar. It sounds like you want to get back to the place where you can just tear it up again.

EC: It's even more nagging than that. The music never stopped. I've been developing and practicing and growing. To design The Stick as an instrument isn't nearly as interesting as to explore it. I never stopped doing that and I do it almost every day. Sometimes I let too much time go by where I don't get to play every day but just in general, I manage to keep my music growing a lot. There was no middle ground where it dropped or stopped. What stopped was getting the music out to the public.

I felt great pressure to come out with an album and even in 1985, when I came out with Parallel Galaxy, *that was way too late for me. I mean, I felt bad not doing it earlier and then there should have been other albums following. I did* Touchboard to Circuitboard *at a time when I was getting into Stick synthesizing. I put it out as a cassette but never really pursued it. The* Hands Across the Board *video came a year later. That was kind of a reward to me from Sal Gutierrez. He lined that up with the people at Warner Bros. Records. Warner Bros. cable TV is where I did that. And then nothing. But it's not like I stopped playing and I am coming back to it now and want to be the musician again. I've been the musician all along. It's more about putting it out in public. That's what I want to do now. That means putting a finishing touch, a polish on it and quit practicing.*

JR: Quit practicing and start playing?

EC: Yeah. To tell you the truth, I go in modes. I'll pick up The Stick on any given day and I might be playing and just enjoying it, just as if I were on stage performing. And then other times I become the nerd, get stuck on one particular thing and I have to practice it and screw up a lot until I really get it. It just goes from one mode to another.

JR: I have to say, and I've told you this before, I used to just love it when I was working down there, I would come into Stick Enterprises early in the morning and you'd be playing in your studio. I'd be in the other room working on the computer or answering emails and just be listening to you play for 45 minutes or a half hour, first thing in the morning. It was absolutely beautiful. One of the most wonderful musical experiences I've had.

EC: How nice. I should tell you that Ben told me the same thing. He worked here afterward and he felt that way about it too. That's nice to hear. Now I don't have anyone that comes by to tell me that they like what they hear (laughs), except for Buckley[32]. He doesn't sing to me like Rushmore[33] used to though. He's not a vocal dog...

JR: What have you learned from your journey so far?

EC: Learning is an enduring part of my life, and I'm a life-long student of scientific literature, but I don't think that's my sole purpose. I like to discover what is hidden and make it known to those around me. Therefore science, and art too, are acquired tools for new discovery. I like the fringes of knowledge and have a novel explanation for most subjects.

JR: What is the motivation to continue refining and creating new Sticks?

EC: A lot of it is plain old customer service, working out of obligation to the community of Stick players. Considering all the detail and custom work, that's a challenge in itself. This service extends to Stick repairs too. It can take a surprising amount of time and labour, reworking Sticks of all vintages to play and sound like our newest ones. I want to move on to my next model with radical new features, but am held back by my daily workload. Recording my own song arrangements and some improvisations might have to wait until retirement, whenever that will be.

JR: What are you grateful for?

---

[32] The family dog, a Standard Poodle, named after Tim.
[33] The Standard Poodle before Buckley.

EC: It's probably more about 'who' than 'what.' Yuta, from age 17, has been my soul mate. We've been together over 54 years and we've done extraordinary things. Without her competence and willing spirit, I could have never established Stick Enterprises, kept production going, dealt with our customers, established the friendships, or even had the space to be musically creative in the first place. We haven't had much help at all, except always from the Stick players themselves. Yuta has been my main source of support on a daily basis, from the beginning.

I find myself saying thank you a lot, for the extraordinary Stick music in all genres and styles, for ardent personal support from Stick players, for publicity and credit coming my way, and to those who offer to blend their creative work with my life's work in various projects. This latter includes your biography of me, Jim, so you have my gratitude too. And there's Greg, a great friend, who has dedicated his exceptional talents and abilities to work closely with Yuta and me (our good fortune). And there's my daughter Grace who heads Stick production and has been with us through thick and thin for almost 30 years. We philosophise and have the most outlandish conversations. And daughter Diana is a constant source of inspiration to me in the esoteric sciences, philosophy, astrology, health and nutrition. And my brother Dan, who from the beginning of Stick Enterprises in 1975, has been conceptualizing our public image with graphics, ads, logos, and later with DVDs and films. And then there's his son Yumi, who is of daily assistance in Stick production and upgrading our computers.

JR: What would your world be like without The Stick?

EC: I think I could have gone in any number of directions. I might have gone into medicine. I might have stayed in the military, but I'm pretty sure I wouldn't have done that. I think about those

252

alternate things. If I'd stayed in the military, I might have gotten in a lot of trouble by being a rebel against the ranks. I would have been outspoken and that would have probably been the end of my career because it's really hard to fight against the team.

In my life, in my mind and in the real world I see things that are in opposition that need to be reconciled and I want to reconcile them. I can see the way to do it. That's stress, stress for everybody around me and stress for me. Sometimes it's entertaining but it adds a real spice and magic. I feel that, in my life and in my mind. It's just there all the time.

And Jim, I know this comment will bring out the journalist in you and that you'll have to ask, "Well, why then this particular direction?"

My answer would have to be, "That's where lightning struck."

Chapter 14 – One Last Story:
The Stick Meets The Log

In 2007, The Stick found a home alongside the Log. Although 'The Log,' the nickname of Les Paul's first solid-body electric guitar, didn't catch on, the instrument that it evolved into, the Gibson Les Paul did and continues to define the solid-body electric guitar. More impressively, Les Paul the musician played and performed with his namesake guitar up until the last days of his life. Paul passed away at age 94 on August 12, 2009. Two years earlier, the Log and The Stick met for the first time on stage at the Iridium Club in New York City.

Les had a regular gig, almost every Monday night, for close to 30 years. His first stay was at a club called Fat Tuesdays and later he landed at *The* Iridium Club. He had various trios backing him up and they did two 90-minute shows each week. Each night he had two or three guests per set, ranging from big celebrities to joke tellers to tap dancers to simply other musicians. It sometimes resembled a vaudeville show. Each guest would get 10-15 minutes. Les always spewed witty lines toward the players. The audience loved the humour. It was 'Schtick' from old showbiz days. Some notable guests included Paul McCartney, Keith Richards, Tony Bennett, Jeff Beck and George Benson. Monday nights with Les Paul was a hot ticket.

Steve Adelson started playing guitar in 1969. In 1983 he heard Emmett demonstrating his Stick at a music expo in Madison Square Garden. Adelson bought his first Stick from Sam Ash Music in Brooklyn, NY, in 1984. Since 1985 he's played Stick exclusively.

"In late 2007, I received an email from my friend and virtuoso guitarist, Muriel Anderson, asking me to join her and meet Les at *The*

Iridium Jazz Club," says Steve. I joined her and she asked Les if I could sit in. He said, 'Sure.' This invite wasn't extended to everyone. I was honoured."

That impromptu meeting was the first of six times that Steve sat in with Les at The Iridium.

"I always played some fast jazz medley to show some chops and then Les would ask for a slow song," Steve continues. "'Sleepwalk' by Santo and Johnny was usually the song of choice. A real crowd pleaser. Les was always friendly. Backstage was a treat. We talked about guitarists like Wes Montgomery and Django Reinhardt. Les knew them personally so his stories about them were very special. On stage, Les would introduce me as the guy with an ironing board with strings. But when I played, he would just stare in amazement. My favourite experience was my first night with Les. Never having heard me before, he asked me to play something (on stage with 250 in attendance). As I'm still playing, maybe a minute into it, he leans over and whispers into my ear, 'You can come back anytime you want.' Wow!

"Les was impressed. He asked me about the design and of course the electronics. He's an innovator so he was naturally curious. He loved the instrument, the techniques and the music that came out of my Stick. He became a fan.

"The trio played mostly jazz standards like 'Sweet Georgia Brown,' so I went with the flow. No Led Zep, or Pink Floyd here. Whenever I played with the band or was a featured solo, I leaned toward his repertoire. A bit of 'Take The Train' or 'Autumn Leaves' was the call of the moment. The audience loved it. Lots of tourists came to see The Les Paul Group, so I was a bonus with my Chapman Stick."

Steve even took some pot shots at the legend.

"As you know," he says, "The Les Paul guitar is made by Gibson. One night Les, in a light-heartedly sarcastic tone, asked what I was holding. Trying to answer with similar sarcasm, I blurted out 'This is a Fender.' Well, the audience playfully booed my comment. I recovered quickly by saying, 'No it's actually a fender from my car, with strings.' It worked. Later, the bassist said she was impressed that I out humoured Les."

(Steve Adelson and his half-fretless Stick. Photo courtesy of Steve.)

The story and the connection with Emmett and The Stick doesn't end there.

Les also told Steve a story of meeting Emmett Chapman, decades earlier, in California. But it had nothing to do with music or instruments or inventing. It turns out that Les was looking to buy a house near The Chapmans, and a mutual friend, Thumbs Carlisle, set up a meeting. Emmett showed Les the house in question, thus temporarily becoming his real estate agent. Emmett confirmed the story and adds, "Yuta, Les Paul and I did a tour of a very elaborate four floor house that was looming above our Yucca Trail home. I thought he might become our next-door neighbour, which would have been very nice. It turned out differently, I guess. So that," Emmett says, "of all things, is my story about Les Paul."

Recognizing the incredible opportunity to reconnect the two, this time for more creative and musical reasons, Steve attempted to set up some communication between Emmett and Les.

"With his permission, I passed Les Paul's email address to Emmett. A message was sent and Les told me he received it but alas, he became ill and passed on soon after. They never connected."

Another missed opportunity. Fortunate happenstance lost. There's still more to the story though. In 2009, *Guitar Player* magazine asked Steve to write a five page story on Emmett. The publishing date kept getting delayed and was finally available for the December 2009 issue in the "Innovator" section. On the cover of this issue was coincidentally, Les Paul. Emmett was supposed to be on that issue's cover, but was understandably bumped for the very appropriate and fitting memorial to Les Paul, who had passed away a few months earlier.

The Stick met the Log on stage. The pictures of Steve playing with Les have a stunning similarity to the pictures of Emmett playing with Barney Kessel. Both Stick players have the ardent look of a humble musician playing with a hero. A perfect beginning to a new musical chapter. Will The Stick usurp the electric guitar as the instrument of choice for budding young rock stars? Maybe one day, maybe not. Regardless, the die has been cast, the train is in motion and the music doesn't appear to be quieting down anytime soon.

Appendix I – New Means of Performance = New Music

"I never really understood Emmett's music until I played with him. Once I was forced to react to where he was going it all made sense."
-Greg Howard

Along with The Stick, one of Emmett's most treasured discoveries is his "Offset Modal Theory." It's a unique, viable and challenging way to approach music and music theory. What follows is a description of his approach to music theory, written by Emmett and published on www.stick.com[34], in response to a request for details that represent his ideas.

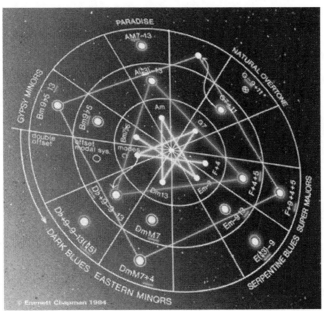

(A visualization of the Offset Modal Theory, by Dan Chapman. Courtesy of Emmett Chapman.)

---

[34] Reprinted here with kind permission.

Both LP and the re-released CD versions of my Parallel Galaxy *album contain the "Wheel" and "Stone" musical charts explaining the entire discovery to those who are inclined toward gaining non-verbal knowledge by way of pattern recognition within closed systems, as with charts encapsulating information in geometric form, in this case patterned after astrology charts. When I finish such a process, I usually become more "verbal" than usual at that point, piling on colorful terms and phrases in an effort to illuminate the discovery.*

On my currently available Galaxy *CD, the triple Wheel chart is on the front cover and the seven faceted Stone chart (set in an unmarked matrix of twelve even divisions) is on the label of the CD itself. I used this system to compose and improvise one of the songs, titled after the* Galaxy *album itself, as a celebration of the discovery and codification of an alternative modal system. It was like discovering a living Garden of Eden, a tempting "paradise" where just one of the physical laws in that universe is off by a twist (as in one of the more famous Star Trek episodes). Since then, the Offset Modal System has grown deeply into my songs and improvs, a musical theory that can be put into practice with unending variation.*

What is this system, I hear you asking (or are you asleep)? It's all contained in seed form on the two charts of the CD and LP. (The third chart, present on the LP version only, is my own horoscope.) Time permitting, I hope to eventually compile my notes into a large book on new music theory for composers and musician improvisers. I should explain that the triple Wheel is a bit of a maze, with the least likely path leading the way out (altering C in a C major scale, of all things)! Then you alter the fifth, a G, to arrive at the "Double Offset Mode" (the outermost of the three Wheels). And then - you never play in C.

260

It's a triple overlay of *Wheel* charts with the traditional Greek modes at the inner one, all seven notes of which are connected by yellow lines in fourth intervals. The middle *Wheel* is the most fruitful, I feel, and displays haunting and exotic modes with chords and scales ascending counter-clockwise, a coherent system of harmonic and scalar movement applicable to any key center (so multiply it all by twelve). The outer *Wheel* "offsets" one more note from the traditional modal system, producing even more exotic and somewhat Arabian constructs. The counter-clockwise *Wheel* is conceptually a top view of a spiral of ascending notes, ranging through as many octaves as you might like to imagine. The matrix is twelve even divisions, as with the twelve equal tempered notes of the octave, the twelfth being known as a major 7th, and the thirteenth being non-existent, in that it's the first tone repeated at the next octave on this spiral staircase. Tone eleven, by the way, is a blue note, the flatted 7th (thanks to Steve Adelson for his pun on Tony Levin's name, used as a song title on his excellent CD album release, The New Sticktet, *featuring Tony together with Steve on that titled song).*

Back to the radial grid. Aligned inside this matrix of twelve points is a symmetrical Stone of seven points, depicting all seven of the altered modal scales simultaneously. As with the Greek modes that still dominate today's music, any note on this chart can be the root of its chord with scale. Chordal movement through all seven of these roots then form an "Offset Modal" relationship in the same manner as with traditional modes. The actual lettered notes are just examples, of course, as you can modulate the whole system to all twelve key centers. Seven notes, any one of which can form a distinctive chord with scale, multiplied by twelve chromatic tones contained in an octave as key or modulation centers, equals 84 modal possibilities.

261

No news here, it's the same amount of permutations as with the familiar Greek modes. Then multiply it all by two to include the same set of possibilities at the outer Wheel, and you have 168 colorful new modes, many of which have been used intuitively but sporadically by inspired classical composers, but without all the interconnections that come with a musical system.

As for the question about my astrological influences and correspondences to this musical theory and practice, astrology was very instrumental in codifying my discoveries. The intervals within chords and scales relate directly to the geometry of angular relationships of zodiacal signs, planets and cusps, (numbers divisible into twelve), possibly even to the evocative moods created by harmonious versus stressful angles (lines respectively marked in blue and red on my musical and astrological charts). There's no doubt I could write several books about these two interwoven subjects of the "Offset Modal System" and the corresponding closed systems of music and astrology. As an astrologer I'm not even a believer, just a practitioner and hobbyist since age 14 or so. Astrology, whether or not it offers any working truth, is a valuable dialectical tool to discover "the geometry of relationships," as I like to put it. The chords with scales in the middle "wheel" come in strangely related pairs, a pair of uplifting "7th chord" scales, a pair of minors as John Coltrane played them, a pair of Middle Eastern major/minor scales, and a "super Lydian" mode with everything raised but the root.

I do have an approach to my OMS that might help you get started on any polyphonic instrument, whether it be frets, keys or The Stick. Here it is in bare form:

Play or arpeggiate a C7 chord with your left hand and find a major scale with your right hand that lowers the 6th and 7th degrees of that scale, including the flatted 6th at Ab and the flatted 7th at Bb. These seven notes then, are your "Single Offset Modal" scale for this particular key. Improvise a melody here, backed by the C7 chord, and try to enjoy the serene balance of some ancient Arabian mood (not allowing current Middle East politics to enter your mind or intrude on tranquility.) This Offset Mode ascends by two whole tones from the C root, and it descends from the root by two whole tones as well - five notes in a row that are related by whole steps.

Now move your left hand down in pitch by two frets and let the Bb7 chord accompany the same 7-tone scale (not changing any melody notes). Reflect on that for a while, as to how the new chord influences your melodic ideas. Then move back and forth between these two 7th chords, four beats to each chord if you like. The C7 chord together with the 7-tone OMS scale spells out a complete C9b13 chord. Seen from Bb7, the combined sound adds up to a Bb9#11 chord.

With your right hand always playing within this same "Offset" scale, move your left hand to F minor6 (it could also be F minor with a natural 7th (also known as "F minor major 7th"). With C7 as the key center (acting as the Roman numeral I chord), you now have enough chords for a song, and can move to the IV chord (F minor6) as a sub-dominant minor, and to the bVII chord (Bb7) as a substitute dominant 7th chord. (In a jazz context, 7th chords with their roots separated by minor 3rds often make good substitution chords, as with Bb7, C#7 and E7 all being interesting substitutes for the dominant G7 in the key of C.)

Extending your left hand to include more of the OMS network of chords at this particular key center of C, move from F minor to its own relative major, Ab major7 (don't change any notes in the right hand). This introduces a super-Lydian scale with every note raised that can be raised, even the 5th degree. Then shift back to F minor, or move parallel from Ab major7 back to Bb7 and back to C7.

So far you've got four OMS chords out of a possible seven in this seven degree network with which to improvise or compose a song. Next I recommend E7, which acts as another substitute dominant 7th chord. It's a III 7th chord and combined with your OMS melody produces a Middle Eastern sounding E b9#9b13 chord.

There are then only two chords still to be found in this network of seven basic chords, where each has a root of one of the seven "Offset" scale degrees (C, D, E, F, G, Ab and Bb). In the left hand we already have C7, E7, F minor, Ab major and Bb7 and all that's left is D minor7b5 (II minor) and G minor7b9b13 (the real dominant 7th or V7 chord in the key of C which can also be played in a G7#9 blues style voicing). This II minor7b5 to V7#9 progression is equivalent to the familiar romantic "turnaround" progression from VII minor7b5 to III7, leading to VI minor or A minor, the relative minor of C.

With these seven chords you can play the Single Offset Modal Network at the middle Wheel on my charts. Then, just for starters using the outer Wheel's Double Offset Mode, you can create an eight-tone scale from the above seven, simply adding a "wild note" that can bend, blues style, from Bb to B. Your C chord, then, can fluctuate from the flatted 7th to a natural 7th - the clichéd call of the siren. Interesting variations then happen at all chords, including a dominant G7 with a major and minor 3rd (for a #9 chord), also the substitute dominant E7 with a perfect 5th.

To broaden the perspective, please keep in mind that your left hand C7 chord need not be the chosen tonic or Roman numeral I chord. Any one of the seven chords can be your home base or "tonic" (with its own Roman numeral I), depending on your mood while improvising or on the song you're composing, whether it be in an altered major, an altered minor or an even more exotic Offset Mode.

An F tonic with the same seven notes accommodates the melodic minor scale. An E tonic creates a flamenco mood with a Middle Eastern color, going from E7 to Fm6 to G7 - lots of combinations and possibilities.

At the next broader view, chromatic transposition multiplies all these possibilities by twelve keys. Your C7 chord with its b13 (or flatted 6th scale degree), and with its wavering 7th degree (borrowed from the outer Double Offset Modal Wheel) can simply be transposed as a block to C# or to D, and so on. Imagine my Triple Wheel chart as a musical game board where you rotate the chromatic lettered notes at an outermost concentric ring.

I wish I could broaden my OMS beyond these boundaries, but there the universe becomes dissolute, expanding faster than light speed, and we're once again alone (lights out). That is, if I "offset" any more modal notes besides the Greek Ionian 1st and 5th degrees, I'm left with a meaningless jumble of chromatic notes. The center simply "will not hold."

And there you have the defined limits, as far as I've explored, of my musical "Parallel Galaxy."

Best to All,

Emmett.

©2001 Emmett Chapman

Appendix II – Free Hands. Finally?

The inspiration was out of pain and hard work. It was like years and years of setting up instruments, and doing fretwork laboriously, like a jeweller. I got involved in the finest kind of fretwork and clearances above each fret so that the setup would be as low as possible and the action as light as possible, the touch as light, the tapping as easy, as fast and as expressive as possible...

This is the first time when I can give the work to someone else..."

The Railboard® – Your Fast Track to Free Hands

-Promotional Video for a new Stick model called 'The Railboard.'

Since the very beginning, since Emmett juggled building those first Sticks with his gigs around LA and travels to New York, tension between Emmett the builder and Emmett the musician has been an ongoing reality. Making the production process and setup of each Stick easier has driven many of the Stick's innovations and advancements from experimenting with different materials like polycarbonate, oak, bamboo and graphite to inventing and refining different hardware components including the Fret Rails, the rear adjustable truss rods and the adjustable Flaps™ dual nut unit. Now literally everything that can be adjustable on The Stick is adjustable. But regardless of those advances and despite having a modestly small, yet dedicated and hardworking staff, since the beginning Emmett has been a part of the manufacturing of every Stick that leaves Stick Enterprises.

Before any Stick leaves Stick Enterprises Emmett inspects it, plays it, does the setup and final adjustments, tweaks it to ensure that all the variables are in place in terms of string height and the even playing surface across all strings and frets for the lightest possible touch and fast, expressive, low action. All these variables work organically together and need to be adjusted in concert. This takes time. The work is meticulous and painstaking. Until only very recently Emmett has done this all himself. Now, daughter Grace, Gary Jibilian and Emmett's nephew Yumi Chapman are all trained to do the preliminary fret dressings and setups after assembly. But Emmett has always been the last stop in The Stick production and often the self-admitted bottleneck at the end of the production line.

The dichotomy, the tension, the pull has always been between Emmett the builder and Emmett the player. The catch is that this opposition has been what made The Stick and Stick Enterprises work. Emmett the builder serves Emmett the musician and vice versa. Since the Freedom Guitar, Emmett the builder's inventions and innovations have been in service of Emmett the musician's quest to play the absolute best instrument to realize his unique two handed string tapping method. The musician's triumphs and struggles have formed and informed the builder's evolution of the instrument. They're two halves of the same whole, symbiotic, two oppositions that Emmett reconciles. A familiar theme in his life.

So, here's the irony: the Free Hands technique, named after Emmett's quest to liberate the hands and create the music of the head and heart only comes from hands that are more than metaphorically chained to the production line of the very instrument intended to set them free. That may be an overly dramatized explanation, but it holds true. Emmett the free musician is beholden to Emmett the builder.

Even though we're not talking about soul-destroying work like drilling holes in rocket parts or dipping those parts in chemical plating baths at Bendix Aviation, Emmett's hands are all too often tied up doing the business and production work of Stick Enterprises, rather than the creative work of an inspired musician.

Now, on the 40th anniversary of Stick Enterprises, all that may have finally changed. After years of design, refinements and prototypes, Stick Enterprises has released a radically new Stick design. Like all truly new Sticks, this one has a new name: The Railboard. They're calling The Railboard 'The Fast Track to Free Hands' for musicians not only because they're less expensive than the wooden Sticks but also because the action and playability is at another scale of precision – lower, more uniform, faster and easier than any Stick to date. In another sense, since all the fretwork happens during the CNC (Computer Numerically Controlled) machining process and is then set in stone with the hard anodizing process, the Railboard just may be Emmett's path towards freeing his hands from the production process. In this sense, the fast track to freeing Emmett's hands to play has taken 40 years.

Emmett has used CNC processes for years to cut the basic Stick structures and fret grooves in the wooden and graphite instruments. This means that the cutting equipment like lathes, milling machines, grinding wheels, and drills are automatically programmed and controlled by a computer. Cuts and millwork are precise and consistently accurate. Of course this saves an enormous amount of time and is really the only practical way to make any kind of mass-produced instrument, even in very small numbers. The Railboard takes this process to the next level by not merely creating the blank for Stick Enterprise to add the frets and other hardware to, but by

268

actually creating the entire fretboard, all the frets included, out of a single piece of hard anodized aluminum.

The Railboard provides for the Stick's, Stick Enterprises' and Emmett's own future but that wasn't Emmett's first realization. "Obviously that's true," he says. "But really I felt like 'why didn't I do this 20 years ago? Why was I slaving so hard when I could have it set in stone with no fretwork at all to do?

"The CNC technology has been around for a good 15-20 years. I was going in that direction with the Fret Rods, then the Fret Rails, which bury their main underlying portions and secure themselves from any vertical displacement. There's been progression in the different models and different materials, injection-moulded polycarbonate, the graphite and even the bamboo is a step in that direction. With the new NS Stick the Rails are only 2/3 the size of our regular ones, so I don't have to shave off the bottom end to make them fit. I'm planning to use the smaller Rails on the next Grand Stick models as well."

The moment of realization that he could integrate the frets into the fretboard and take away the need to do all the filing and fretwork also happened in stages. The first idea was to create an integrated fretboard piece that was like a piece of hardware about a quarter of an inch thick that would screw, bolt or even affix itself with adhesive onto a wooden neck. "My first two prototypes I built about four years ago are built that way," says Emmett. "I still have them. In fact, I'm probably going to sell one of them. The problem was that it wasn't as stable because there's two different materials involved, so expansion and humidity affected the hardwood and anodized aluminum differently. It was pretty good, but nothing like the Railboard now, which just stays the way you set it up. The action is so low you can barely see the clearance uniformly above each fret. That's really made the difference.

"It got to the prototype stage where I liked it well enough. That piece of hardware affixed to a wooden neck was pretty nice. It looked good too but it just didn't have the precision and I ended up having to do a lot of the manual fret filling and crowning like I'd always done. So I figured the way to do it was to make a one-piece integrated neck and fingerboard with Rails all together cut from one piece of aluminum. Then, the most important part of the process was to have a CNC program do the kind of cuts that I had been doing by hand and make them uniform. After everything is done, the fly-cutter comes over the top and shaves down a small amount off of the fret tops, all in one cut to form a straight and even plane of playing surface. That way it's one command, one cut.

"The second part was to create relief under the bass strings at the lower pitched frets, because of the thick bass strings. Instead of a flat cutter I needed a ball end cutter that had a radius programmed on it that would do a shallow cut, an elongated oval depression that provides relief under the bass strings at the centre position. I fine tuned it a couple of times and now every instrument is cut uniformly and they're hard anodized so there's nothing more I can do – even if I wanted to. I'm not even tempted to do any fine-tuning though, they're that good.

"Finally, just for a little insurance that's so subtle you wouldn't even see it with the naked eye, there's a divided adjustable truss rod on the rear side that allows me to add just the tiniest bit of relief to the lower pitch half while maintaining a straight profile to the higher pitched half, to compliment the relief I created in the middle under the bass strings.

270

"I took two finished instruments, a blue one and a black one and gave them the sun test. I let them sit in the sun for hours. When I took them back inside they were too hot to touch, and the strings went a little sharp, but the overall profile didn't warp. They were still solid. We're now in our third run and the musical and sales results have been beyond my expectations. And sure enough, my work is minimal."

With six distinctly different models of wooden Sticks and the NS Stick, Stick Enterprises has no intention of replacing wooden instrument production with The Railboard, as was attempted in the '80s with the polycarbonate Sticks. "The intention with the Railboard was to have a new model that was really high tech and incorporated my own personal wish list of features," says Emmett. "But we have a huge inventory of hardwoods. We've added laminated ash recently and more bamboo from China. We don't have any intention of terminating wooden production. It's too popular, too successful. People have their favourite types of Sticks, but I must say that the Railboard sure makes my job and my music a lot easier."

He seems to have hit all the items on his personal wish list of features. The Railboard is the only Stick Emmett is currently playing, although that's a bit misleading. "I always just played one instrument," he says. "Now it's the Railboard, but I've always just played one instrument, until I change to the next one. I've never had two different models going at the same time."

Once again, one wonders if there are any more next steps in The Stick's evolution?

"Yes," says Emmett. "I've got three or four different processes I'm exploring, different surface coatings. I'm trying chrome, which can be very hard. There are possibilities for metal plasma coatings that are used in aerospace that are very exotic but very expensive. There are ceramic coatings, other possibilities. It just turns out that the aluminum oxide is as hard as sapphire, harder than tooled steel.

"Here's something," he continues. "We've just finished our experimentation with glow powder of various colours. We mix the powder with liquid epoxy and pour it into the position marker 'bowls.' It dries slowly and forms very level. It looks beautiful and really glows like mad. Aqua is the brightest colour. Blues and greens are working well too. That's the latest little compatible feature to go with the instrument. Some things are just nice and work with the design instead of fighting the design. For many customers we're going to fill the position marker holes. On all Railboards with the linear inlay, the markers will either be the same colour as the aluminum oxide or filled with glow powder."

The evolution continues. Free Hands evolve...

With Much Thanks

There are many, many people without whom this project would never have seen the light of day. I hope to catch most of you with the few short words below, realizing that words can't come close to expressing my gratitude. For those I miss, I apologize in advance but please realize that any omission was unintentional.

First and foremost, thank you to Greg Howard for planting the seed, whether he realized it or not, that became this book. Greg has been an inspiration to me, not just as a world-class musician but also as a true creative spirit and caring, supportive friend.

Without the enthusiastic support and encouragement of Dr. George Johnson at Thompson Rivers University in Kamloops, British Columbia, this book would have never even been conceived. Thanks to all who read, made comments and helped to edit earlier drafts, most notably to my colleague Heather Haxton for her outstanding editing and proofreading and to Val Webber for her keen teacher eyes.

Thank you to the overwhelming number of Stick players, many of whose words and works are represented here. I have yet to meet a Stick player I don't like (true story). Thank you for sharing your stories, your music, your knowledge and your inspiration with me. Many players I have met over the years have become friends and contributed to this work, (often unintentionally) notably, Glenn Poorman, Jim Meyer, Qua Veda, Bob Culbertson, Don Schiff, Steve Adelson, James Charbonneau, Matt Tate, Tom Griesgraber, Virna Splendore, Louis Hesselt-van-Dinter, Scott Schurr and many others who although aren't named, are no less appreciated.

I must thank brother Dan, his lovely wife Yuki and sons Yumi and Dean. Dan opened his vaults and shared his work with me, holding back nothing. His family opened their home to me – I've never slept on a more comfortable couch or eaten better sushi. Dan was an invaluable sounding board for ideas, provided most of the images in this book, was an early editor of previous drafts, created the book's cover and worked tirelessly with me whenever I needed help, as he's done on many other Stick projects. His documentary[35] *Emmett* was an invaluable reference source that he generously provided.

Thanks to my lovely wife Lori who gave me the time, space and perfectly timed pushes (not so subtly sometimes) to finish this project. Without her support, belief and recognition of the importance of this work to me, I am certain that I would never have finished.

Finally, for more than words can repay, I thank Emmett and Yuta for sharing their lives with me. I hope, with gratitude and humility, that I got it right and even though it's impossible to really convey the importance and magnitude of what you've been able to accomplish and the gifts you've given the world, I hope I've been able to add a small piece to that picture and help to ensure The Stick's and your legacy.

---

[35] In production at time of this publication.

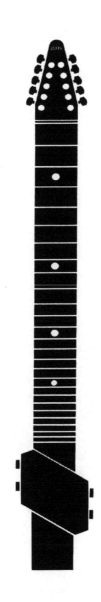

About the Author

Jim Reilly is a writer, journalist, musician and teacher currently living in Calgary, Alberta, Canada. His first Stick, #492 Oak Grand Stick grouped into seven melody and five bass strings arrived on December 17, 1993 at about 11:30 am. (In truth, he was a Stick player long before that, but that's a story for another day.) His first thought as he opened up the white, hardshell flight case and looked down on his new instrument was, "What the hell have I gotten myself into now?" Over the years, he's played oak, ironwood and graphite Sticks. His main instrument now is a prototype model that was made in conjunction with the German company BassLab. The BassLab Sticks never went into full production.

(In performance at Stick Night concert. Screen shot courtesy of Dan Chapman)

Since 1993, Jim has played Stick across North America, hosted and taught at Stick seminars, demoed instruments at NAMM Shows in Anaheim, California and been featured on CBC Radio One in Canada. His writing has been featured in several music magazines and online. His short novel, *The Bass Player*, is currently available from all the usual sources. He can be found on Facebook (search Jim Reilly Creative) and reached by email at twohandedpress@gmail.com.

Made in the USA
San Bernardino, CA
13 August 2019